Better Homes
& Gardens

celebrate the
SEASON®
2017

Let It SNOW

contents

fall

trims

food

gifts

118 No matter if you're at home in the kitchen or at the crafts table, this creative chapter will inspire you to make unforgettable gifts. And not only will you have fun doing what you love, but you'll also make the season a whole lot brighter for loved ones.

kids

138 Kids will love learning a few new tricks—repurposing and crafting techniques they'll have a blast mastering. A selection of adorable projects will teach children how to paint, cut, dye, stamp, and more as they make fun holiday trims and gifts.

in a twinkling

Put a lot of heart, not a lot of time, into these clever seasonal surprises.

Better Homes & Gardens

MEREDITH CONSUMER MARKETING
Consumer Marketing Product Director: Heather Sorensen
Consumer Marketing Product Manager: Wendy Merical
Consumer Marketing Billing/Renewal Manager: Tami Perkins
Business Manager: Diane Umland
Senior Production Manager: Al Rodruck

WATERBURY PUBLICATIONS, INC.
Editorial Director: Lisa Kingsley
Creative Director: Ken Carlson
Associate Editors: Tricia Bergman, Mary Williams
Associate Design Director: Doug Samuelson
Production Assistant: Mindy Samuelson
Contributing Editor: Sue Banker
Contributing Copy Editor: Terri Fredrickson
Contributing Proofreader: Linda Wagner

BETTER HOMES & GARDENS® MAGAZINE
Editor in Chief: Stephen Orr
Executive Editor: Oma Blaise Ford
Managing Editor: Gregory H. Kayko
Creative Director: Jennifer D. Madara
Senior Deputy Editor, Food and Entertaining: Nancy Wall Hopkins

MEREDITH NATIONAL MEDIA GROUP
President: Tom Harty

MEREDITH CORPORATION
Chairman and Chief Executive Officer: Stephen M. Lacy

In Memoriam: E.T. Meredith III (1933–2003)

old traditions, new inspirations

There are some holiday traditions I cling to. I absolutely love going to church on Christmas Eve. The candlelight, carols, and spirit that fill the sanctuary also fill my heart.

I thoroughly enjoy baking cutout sugar cookies. My daughter and I can spend hours chatting and laughing as we create all kinds of holiday characters and seasonal shapes.

I'm like a little kid anticipating the ritual of putting up the tree. All of the ornaments have stories—some of the best stem from those that are lovingly handmade.

And I take great delight in wrapping up the gifts I've made for family and friends. They are my most favorite gifts to give.

Yet along with the traditions I hold dear, every year I like to shake things up a bit. Maybe it's something fresh for the front door or a new recipe or two to share with guests. And I often give a new crafting technique a whirl—especially if it will make that "just-right" gift. So while I do hang on tightly to the traditions I love, I also find new inspiration along the way.

That's why I want to share *Better Homes & Gardens CELEBRATE THE SEASON* with you. This book is an awesome source of inspiration for festive crafts projects, incredible recipes, handcrafted gifts, and amazing party ideas that will add joy to your holiday season.

So enjoy new holiday ideas offered in *CELEBRATE THE SEASON*. And don't be surprised if some of these ideas become favorite and cherished traditions.

The merriest of holidays to you!

Sue Barker

fall

Bring it on! Bold colors, textural accents, and seasonal symbols make inviting autumn accents for the home.

Paisley Panache

The ever-loved paisley pattern has graced home decor items and wearables for centuries. Use stitches, paints, and sewing trims to freshen this familiar favorite.

AUTUMNAL GREETING

It only takes a few embroidery stitches to make this paper paisley pop. Use the pattern on page 152 to cut a paisley shape from scrapbook paper. Place the paisley on corrugated cardboard; use a sewing needle to poke holes approximately ¼ inch apart and ¼ inch from the edge. Use embroidery floss to trim edge with buttonhole stitches. Create a flower using straight stitches and French knots, prepoking holes as you work. Attach paisley to the front of a notecard using glue dots. Stitch a bottom border on the card if desired.

SHAPELY PLACE MAT

Break away from traditional place mat shapes with something a little unexpected. Placed across from one another, sets of paisley-shape place mats create a fun rolling wave along a tabletop's center. Enlarge the pattern on page 153. Cut two 22×16-inch rectangles from paisley fabric using different fabrics to make the mat reversible. With wrong sides facing, use fusible web to bond the two fabric pieces together. Use the pattern to cut out the paisley shape. Machine-stitch binding around the edge.

POSH PILLOW

Muted paisley decorator fabric makes a pretty pillow. Bump it up a notch with contrasting embroidery stitches and buttons accenting a focal paisley. Cut two 14×16-inch pieces from decorator fabric, with a paisley centered on one piece for the pillow front. Use desired stitches and embroidery floss to embellish the design, adding buttons around the edge. With right sides facing and using ½-inch seams, sew the pillow front to back, leaving an opening to turn. Clip corners and turn. Stuff the pillow with fiberfill and hand-sew the opening closed.

UPCYCLED ART

Turn your junk drawer into a fabulous work of art! This dimensional paisley piece incorporates empty tape rolls, wood beads, poker chips, golf tees, toy parts, kitchen gadgets, and more. Start by spray-painting a 16×20-inch artist's canvas black; let dry. Enlarge the paisley pattern on page 153; cut out. Center the pattern on the canvas and draw around it with white marking pencil. Use strong glue to attach pieces to the canvas, starting with the paisley outline. Use rounded shapes, such as poker chips, to form a scalloped edge. Continue adding and layering pieces to create the desired pattern and border. Let the glue dry. Spray-paint the dimensional pieces black; let dry. Use a paintbrush and acrylic paint to add color to the pieces. Use very little paint on the brush and only apply it to the tops of the pieces, allowing the undersides to remain black. When dry, brush a very light coat of white along some of the edges for definition. Let the paint dry and spray with clear polyurethane.

Turkey Time

Celebrate the season of thanks with charming postcard accents that hint at yesteryear. Find the treasures in antiques stores, or print images from the Internet onto cardstock.

GUEST GIFT

Embellish each place setting with a different postcard tucked into a pinecone "stand" to mimic a work of art on an easel.

INVITING PLACE SETTING

Autumnal colors, vintage postcard accents, and seasonal naturals blend together for a most welcoming Thanksgiving table.

CLEVER CANDLEHOLDER

Clear vessels reveal and protect postcard art. Place a candle in the center of the vessel and fill with colored popcorn or dried beans. Tuck in a postcard on each side for viewing all around. Keep the flame away from postcard and filler. Never leave a burning candle unattended.

PERSONALIZED PLACE MAT

Here's a place card, meaningful message, and place mat all rolled into one. Scanned postcards, or those saved from the Internet, work easily into a grid design to print on 11×17-inch cardstock. Personalize the place mats with guests' names and personalized messages saying why you are thankful for them. If your home printer doesn't print 11×17-inch paper, upload the file to a local print shop or adhere individual pieces onto the cardstock using a glue stick.

TIMELY
NAPKIN RINGS

Share Thanksgiving greetings on napkin rings. Choose plain round rings and cut strips from postcard copies to fit. Attach strips to rings using strong double-sided tape.

Thanksgiving Greetin

For wealth of harvest,
For basket and store,
For joy and for rest
We thank Thee once more.

GOODIE JARS

Do family and friends a favor in the season of giving. Fill jars with a favorite salty-sweet combo and trim the jar with a postcard clipping. Back the postcard art with scrapbook paper and trim a narrow border. Attach the artwork to the jar using strong double-sided tape or glue dots.

SEASONAL SALUTATIONS

Send thoughtful messages or dinner invitations this Thanksgiving with handmade greeting cards. Fold a piece of scrapbook paper in half to make card base. Trim the bottom with a decorative-edge scissor. Use scrapbook paper to back a section cut out from a postcard copy and attach with double-sided tape.

Copper Tones

Warm metallic hues are easy to love and don't cost a pretty penny when you rely on hardware and crafts store supplies.

FOILED AGAIN

Copper foil tape is an electrician's staple. It quickly fancies up vases and the edge of an unfinished shelf. A rugged tree slice gets a brilliant makeover when layered with copper leaf. Generously apply gilding adhesive and copper sheets to the flat surface until there is consistent coverage and shine. For an aged effect, apply fewer metal sheets and let some wood grain show.

SHELF UPGRADE

Basic brackets become lovely accents when treated with metallic spray paint. Apply three light coats for a thorough, durable finish—and don't forget to spray all screwheads.

SHINY SILHOUETTE

Here's an old-fashioned idea with a newfangled look. Trace a pretty profile onto a thin sheet of copper using a fine-point permanent marking pen, then carefully cut out the image using detail scissors. Sketch a floral background on thick crafts paper with a metallic paint pen and attach the head-turning likeness with construction adhesive.

PIPE DREAMS

Spend some time in the plumbing aisle combining pipe and elbows to fashion a table base as shown in Photos A and B. Pipe can be cut at most home improvement stores, or do it yourself with a pipe cutter. Connect the base to the tabletop with U clamps. To keep copper pipe bright and shiny, finish it to stop oxidation. Sand the metal with emery paper, then seal it with spray polyurethane.

GRIT AND GLITZ

Get the look of a custom headboard by installing laminate flooring on ¼-inch plywood cut to span the bed. Cut hardboard strips to match the flooring pattern, wrap them in thin 36-gauge copper sheets, and affix them with construction adhesive. A frame of white trim with miter-cut corners finishes the piece, which is hung on the wall with a French cleat.

FANCY FEET

Take a console table from fine enough to fancy. Wrap wide painters tape 6 inches from the bottom of each leg and spray leg below tape with a coat of primer for glossy surfaces; let dry. Spray on two coats of copper spray paint and let dry.

AT YOUR SERVICE

Make an entry butler from an 11×16-inch wood slice and an array of hardware and hardware store standards that function as clamps for test tube vases and a hang bar outfitted with S hooks.

Spell It Out

Around your neck or around your house, letters and words get messages across beautifully.

CHARMING CHOKER

Check out the jewelry section at the crafts store for a selection of charms touting letters and words. Find a couple that are meaningful to you and slide them onto a chain. For seasonal flair, thread through a sheer narrow ribbon in an autumnal hue. Knot each ribbon end to the end of the chain for easy on and off.

WONDERFUL WORDS WALL PIECE

Wood plaques are in and this pretty wall piece will show off your artistic side, whether or not you thought you had one. Start with a plaque from the crafts store. With boards running horizontally, paint simple flowers and leaves in the upper left and lower right corners as shown using acrylic paint colors that coordinate with your decor. Using the board lines as a guide, paint "feeling" with black as shown; let dry. Using very little white on a small round paintbrush, paint the inside of each letter. Using wood letters that spell out "thankful." paint them white and let dry. Use wood glue to adhere the letters in place; let dry.

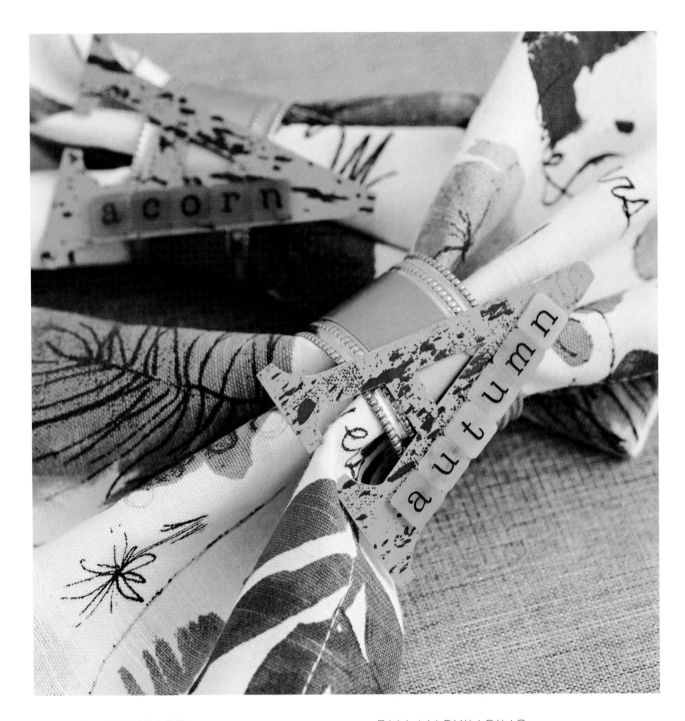

SEASONAL HEART

Available in crafts stores, game letters add fun to home decorations. Choose words indicative of the fall season or other words that are meaningful to you. Glue the words to a precut plaque, adding dimensional scrapbooking flower accents. To soften the look of letters on a whitewashed background, brush the letter edges with white paint and let dry.

FALL NAPKIN RING

Give plain napkin rings a fall facelift in no time. Use double-sided tape to add a colorful piece of ribbon to the napkin ring. A simple letter can be used in lieu of a place card. Or, for a more seasonal approach, hot-glue a large metal "A" onto the ring and add a seasonal word along one edge.

Take a Seat

Give chairs and benches, even worn ones, a fresh new look with a few simple techniques.

SMOOTH TRANSITION

Give a shapely chair a new attitude with fabric. Remove legs, and put the chair on a protected table. Place fabric over the chair, smooth it flat. Cut fabric roughly the shape of the chair, leaving a border of approximately 2 inches all around the chair. Apply a thick layer of decoupage medium to the fabric; it will soak through and cling to the chair and stiffen as it dries. Trim the fabric again, leaving about 1 inch of excess as shown in Photo A. Brush on a second coat of decoupage medium; let dry. Using a pen, trace the chair's edge on the wrong side of the fabric. Hold a piece of light cardboard against the right side of the fabric to steady the pen. Carefully cut along the line as shown in Photo B. Seal the seat and edges with a final coat of decoupage medium and let dry. Spray-paint the legs gold; reattach when dry.

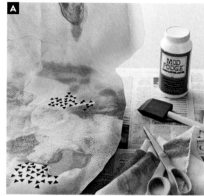

CHERISHED CHAIR

Save a worn-out rattan chair from the junk pile and use your creativity to give it new life. Remove the old rattan from the seat and wrap black twine around the seat frame from front to back. Weave contrasting twines under and over the black twine as shown. Use chunky yarns to cross-stitch a floral design onto the intact rattan on the chairback. For basic cross-stitch stitches, see page 157.

KNOW THE DRILL BENCH

X marks the spot on a wooden bed frame-turned-bench that's adorned with simple cross-stitches. Using a drill bit sized larger than paracord, mark and drill an 8×14-inch grid of holes through the bench back, spacing the holes about 1 inch apart like a pegboard. Stitch in the desired pattern. For ease in stitching and to prevent fraying, tape a sewing needle to the end of the paracord. For a modern Scandinavian style, limit the palette to three colors of paracord.

Everything's Coming Up Cattails

UPSTANDING CORNUCOPIA

Thanksgiving guests will love being greeted by this handsome arrangement. To make it, place a wedge of floral foam in the bottom of a cornucopia. Carefully poke in preserved cattail stems, spacing so they do not touch. Fill in with dried flowers. Add a ribbon bow in seasonal colors as the grand finale.

ROOM-TO-GROW PICTURE TRIO

Create a striking wall arrangement to enjoy during the fall months. Remove the glass from three 5×7-inch photo frames. For each frame, cut a piece of scrapbook paper, in seasonal colors, to fit. Hot-glue an artificial leaf to paper, trimming leaf edges even with paper. Place in frame. Cut three long-stemmed preserved cattails into thirds as shown in photo; hot-glue inside frames aligning stems. Hang vertically.

ELEGANTLY STATED

Make a meal extra special with mini cattails gracing each place setting. Cushion the seasonal accent with a pretty cloth napkin and tie with colorful ribbons.

ALL-NATURAL TABLE TRIMS

Small log chunks make natural bases for displaying preserved cattails. For each decoration, drill a deep hole in the top of the log piece, slightly larger than the cattail stem. Cut cattail to desired size and slide into log. Tie the stem with a jute bow.

PUMPKIN SURPRISE

Quick as a wink to complete, this pumpkin decoration makes a big impact. Cut three preserved cattail stems in staggering lengths. Drill holes, smaller than the cattail stems, into the pumpkin top in triangle formation. Thread a couple of large wood beads on the stem bottoms and poke into pumpkin. Top each cattail with a small wood bead.

trims

WELCOMING AND WONDROUS
Warm hearts and excite spirits with
handcrafted holiday decorations that
create a most merry atmosphere.

Warm Welcomes

Greet guests with something unexpected at the front door—bright and cheery decorations that rival rings of greenery.

JINGLE TREE

Pretty to look at and fun to hear, this sparkling tree spreads the spirit of the season. To make the base, cut three sections from 1½-inch-wide flat wood trim: a 12-inch-long trunk, a 6½-inch long top cross bar, and a 10½-inch long bottom cross bar. Use construction adhesive to glue the top cross bar 3½ inches from one end of the trunk piece and the bottom cross bar 4 inches from the opposite end; let dry. To hang, drill two holes ¼ inch apart in the trunk piece, 1 inch from top. Thread with wire and make a loop for hanging; knot wire ends. Paint the wood base silver; let dry. A set of six 3½-inch tart pans holds the jingle bells. For each tart pan, use strong, clear adhesive, such as E6000. Fill the bottom of the tart pan with the adhesive and put a single layer of jingle bells in silver, turquoise, and white. Continue adding layers in this manner until the tart pan is full of bells. For the top layer, arrange so the tops of the jingle bells are exposed. Let the adhesive set thoroughly. Adhere the tart pans to the wood base as shown. Add three large bells to the trunk.

TIN TRIMS

Single tart pans make showy ornaments. Add jingle bells as for the tree and glue a cording hanger to the back.

ALL THAT GLITTERS

A shimmering snowflake ring encircles a bold holiday message. For the base, use an 18-inch diameter flat wood wreath form. Paint the form white and let it dry. Use precut wood or plastic shapes for the 9-inch letters and snowflakes. Purchase white shapes or paint them white and let dry. To add glitter to each shape, brush the front with decoupage medium and sprinkle with glitter; let dry. Tie a ribbon hanger to the wreath form. Use strong all-weather clear adhesive to attach the letters to the wreath form and to each other. Glue the snowflakes to the wreath as shown.

LANDING PLACE

A snow-laden branch draws a colorful flock to this front door sensation. Start with a fallen limb, approximately 24 inches long. A limb that has several small branches stemming from it lends room for a larger collection of plastic and feathered bird ornaments. To give the appearance of snow, brush the branch tops with white paint; let dry. Wire the birds to the branch. Do not use glass ornaments unless the display is going to be hung inside. Tie a wide ribbon bow to the bottom of the branch.

WHAT A CARD

Give Christmas cards a second go-round by transforming them into a colorful wreath. Start with a 12-inch-diameter flat wood wreath form and six 5-inch-diameter wood plaques. Paint the wood pieces white and let dry. Cut six circles from cards to fit plaque tops; hot-glue in place. If desired, use layers of card pieces to cover plaque tops. Hot-glue garland trim around each wood round. Use construction adhesive to attach wood rounds to wreath form, keeping card images upright. Hot-glue a bow to the lower right. Use a staple gun to attach ribbon to the back of the wreath for hanging.

JOLLY JUMBO POSTCARD

A vintage postcard gets mega exposure when enlarged to twice its size. Make an enlarged photocopy of an original postcard or of one off the Internet; print on cardstock and trim excess. Use glue stick to adhere the cutout to contrasting cardstock; trim a narrow border. Adhere to textured gold cardstock and trim a 1-inch border. Use an oversized clip to hang the piece of nostalgia on the door. To hang the clip, use temporary wall mount strips or drill a hole in the clip and hang it on a nail.

A Jolly Good Christmas.

COOKIE CREW

Visitors will look twice at this door decor that's inspired by holiday baking. To make the gingerbread guys and gals, use air-dry clay in terra-cotta color. To flatten, place clay between sheets of waxed paper as shown in Photo A. Flatten to about ¼ inch using a rolling pin. Remove the top sheet of waxed paper and use a cookie cutter to cut out the gingerbread shape as shown in Photo B. Cut out approximately eight cookies; let air dry. Use acrylic paint and buttons to add details to the clay shapes as shown in Photo C. Use hot glue to adhere the buttons. Use all-weather strong clear adhesive to attach the cookies to a cooling rack or onto the tops of wrapped gifts. Tie a ribbon bow at the top of the rack, slipping a wooden spoon through the center.

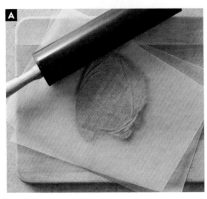

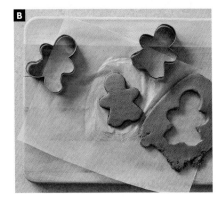

Frosty Trims

Capture the magical look of crackled ice with stunning trims crafted from plastic ceiling tiles.

SHEET OF ICE

Paired with cool blue, a clear ceiling tile place mat lends wintry appeal. To cut a ceiling tile to the desired size, place the tile on a protected surface and score it using a metal yardstick and utility knife. Use slight pressure to carefully score the tile again and again until cut through. Sand the edges smooth. Trim the mat with snowflake stickers. For a take-home gift for guests, place a snowflake ornament to the side of the mat. If not using a tablecloth, prevent scratching by placing clear plastic bumpers on the back of the mat.

ALL AGLOW

Flickering candlelight looks gorgeous reflecting off crystal-like textures. To make the candle ring, cut an 8×22-inch piece from a flexible ceiling tile using the same method as for the place mat. Wearing work gloves and protective eyewear, bring the short ends of the ceiling tile together. If the tile is too stiff to do this, do not use it for this project. If the tile bends easily, then it will work well for a candle ring. On one short end, put a line of strong, clear adhesive on the smooth side of the ceiling tile about ¼ inch from the edge. Make the ring, overlapping the ends ½ inch; clamp each end to hold. While glue is bonding, add a variety of ribbons around the candle ring, overlapping ends 1½ inches and securing with hot glue. This will help the ring keep its shape while the adhesive is drying. Be sure the adhesive is thoroughly set before removing the clamps.

IN A FLURRY

Add to the winter wonderland with temporary glass additions. Adorn each guest's glass with a pair of adhesive snowflakes to carry out the theme.

ASSIGNED SEATING

Make fancy place cards glittery with trims and stickers. Start with a 4×4½-inch piece of ceiling tile. Cut a 3-inch square from turquoise glitter paper. Attach the paper square to the ceiling tile piece ½ inch from the right edge and centered top to bottom using double-sided tape. Press on an adhesive gemmed letter to the paper. Hot-glue ribbon to the left side of the place card; add an adhesive snowflake. To make the place card stand, cut a 2½-inch square from ceiling tile, then cut again from opposite corners. This will make two stands. Hot-glue a stand to the center back of each place card.

CLEARLY CHRISTMAS

Keep the tree trims light and airy using small rectangles cut from ceiling tiles as mini canvases. Press on holiday stickers and trim with metallic silver pipe cleaners, and these decorations are ready to hang.

PERSONALITY PLUS

Bring on the smiles with snowmen (or gals!). Cut an ice-like ceiling tile to the desired size using a metal yardstick and utility knife on a protected surface. Sand the edges smooth. Carefully drill a hole at each top corner, approximately 2 inches in from each edge. On the smooth side, paint a simple black outline of a snowperson using the photo for inspiration. Add a few circles for snow. Let the paint dry. Paint in the remainder of the picture; let dry. Thread ribbon through the holes for hanging.

Playful Palette

Traditional red and white pair with turquoise for a holiday color scheme that's fun and fresh. While some of these trims cater to kids, there are also sophisticated accents so everyone has something to love.

WARM HEARTS, COLD HANDS

Turn your imagination loose while crafting snow friends to bring joy all winter. Not only do these characters elicit smiles, but they also do their fair share in recycling. While these bodies are made of empty aerosol cans, you can use other empty containers as well. If the container is lightweight, fill it with sand to prevent tipping. If using an aerosol can, pull off and discard the spray nozzle. Use hot glue to adhere the end of bulky natural yarn at the base of the can. Wrap the yarn around the can, adding spots of glue every so often to secure it in place. When the can is completely covered, clip the yarn and glue the end in place. Press a plastic foam ball onto the top of the can for the head; use hot glue to secure it in place. Cover the ball with yarn as done for the can. Shape arms and hands from chenille stems. Tuck the ends under the yarn and secure with hot glue. Use beads for the face and a tiny coil of orange chenille stem for the nose. Natural chenille stems add dimensional eyebrows and mustaches. Trim each character as desired using items such as buttons, felt, ribbon, and doll hats.

ADORABLE APPLIQUÉ

A playful wall hanging creates big impact using fun fabrics and fonts. While this quilted piece is 25×30 inches with 5-inch-tall letters, you can easily make it smaller or larger by simply adjusting the letter size and borders. To make the letters, print out the desired letters on a printer; cut out. Turn the letters over and trace onto the paper side of some fusible webbing. Cut around the shapes approximately ¼ inch outside the lines; iron to the wrong side of the desired letter fabric following the manufacturer's instructions. Cut out the letters. Peel the paper off the back of each letter and iron in place on background fabric. The letters should be adhered to the background well enough that they don't lift. With thread that matches the letter color, start with a tacking stitch. Using a clear presser foot, align your shape right in the middle of your presser foot so that your needle sinks at the edge. Take a few very small straight stitches along the edge of the shape to help secure the following zigzag stitches. Zigzag around each letter, aligning so that stitches are all on the shape and just barely coming off the edge into the background piece. At corners, drop the needle and pivot. On curves, sink the needle and pivot slowly and gradually. Finish with a tacking stitch. For borders, add side strips, then top and bottom strips. Sandwich a thin batting sheet between the front and a backing piece; quilt the piece using matching thread and free-motion quilting or as desired. Bind the edge and add hanging tabs if you wish to hang the wall piece from a rod.

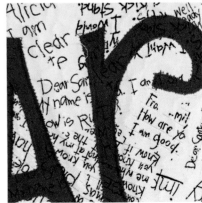

MERRY MANTEL

Here's a great way to keep off-season art under wraps—literally! Choose wrapping paper that coordinates with your color scheme and wrap framed pieces or canvases, adding ribbon bow accents. Foam board, plywood, boxes, cardboard, or blank canvases can also be used for the faux gifts.

SQUARE-TOED STOCKINGS

L-shape stockings zap the mantel with color. Varying the cuff trims makes each one unique. To make one, trace and enlarge the stocking pattern on page 154; cut out. For stocking front, piece together 2½-inch fabric squares checkerboard style. Cut one stocking front, one back, two lining pieces, one from fusible webbing, and one from fleece. Cut a 2×10-inch hanging loop and an 8×16½-inch cuff. Sandwich the fleece between the stocking front and lining piece; pin together. Stitch a grid pattern (¼ inch from each seam) through all layers. Following the manufacturer's instructions, iron the fusible webbing to the wrong side of the stocking back. Place the lining piece onto the fusible webbing; pin in place. With right sides together, sew stocking back to front using ¼-inch seams; leave top open. Trim seams; clip curves; turn right side out. For cuff, stitch rickrack or other trims along one long edge as shown in photo. With right sides facing, sew the 8-inch edges together. Fold cuff in half lengthwise with wrong sides together, matching raw edges and seams; press. Slip tube inside stocking top, with trim against stocking and aligning raw edges; stitch together. Fold cuff to outside. Press under ½ inch on both long edges of 2×10-inch piece. Fold in half lengthwise, bringing folded edges together and enclosing the raw edges; press; edge-stitch. Fold strip in half; sew to the top left corner of stocking.

SLEIGH BELL WREATH

A flocked wreath is truly elegant with the addition of large jingle bells dangling from a bright red ribbon bow. Tie three jingle bells to the ends of cording. If cording is too thick to thread through bells, use strong clear adhesive. Arrange the cords to hang from the wreath at varying lengths; knot ends together and trim excess cord. Wire the knot to the upper right portion of the wreath. Tie a ribbon bow around the knot.

HEAVENLY DETAILS

Jazz up plain plastic ornaments with velvet ribbon bows and trims from a crafts store's jewelry and scrapbooking departments. Because the trims are hot-glued in place, glass ornaments are not recommended.

BOBECHE ORNAMENTS

Decorative glass candle collars get a new use as tree ornaments. For each trim, use pinking shears to cut a circle from felt large enough to cover the center opening. Hot-glue in place. Glue a charm frame onto the felt, adding a button or other tiny trim in the center. Thread metallic cording through the charm ring to hang.

GOOD TOSS

Perk up decor with toss pillows that carry out the playful theme. Simply striped or created like the wallhanging on page 49, these pillows look just as good on a bed as they do on a couch. If your sewing machine does embroidery, consider personalizing a pillow top with a fun phrase. For a super-soft pillow back, chenille fabric can't be beat.

GOODIES ON THE GO

A pint-size tree makes the perfect holder for party favor bags. To hang surprise bags from the tree branches, fold over the top of a decorative bag and secure with a holiday sticker. Punch holes in the corners and add a metallic silver pipe cleaner handle. Hot-glue a bow to one side for a festive finish. Hang the bags on the tree and fill in with candy canes spruced up with ribbon bows.

OH-SO-JOLLY TABLETOP

Choose two or three colors for the palette and all the decorations will complement each other. Keep the colors in mind as you shop for candies, drinks, dishes, and more. You'll find it an easy challenge and the results will be truly delightful.

Trims

SWEET TOUCH

Keep candlelight contained in clear glass vessels. Choose those that leave some room around the candle and fill halfway with wrapped holiday candies.

MERRY MESSAGES

Turn to the crafts store for small wood cutouts to rest at each guest's place at the table. Leave the wood unfinished or paint as desired.

OLD-FASHIONED FUN

Santa mugs make each place at the table more than merry. Filled with out-of-the-ordinary candies and cocoa mix, guests will love taking these treasures home.

SNOWFLAKE TABLE TOPPER

A gigantic snowflake adds shapely cutouts to the tabletop. Use soft nonadhesive interfacing to fold and cut the snowflake in the same manner as you would paper snowflakes. Iron the cutout flat using a pressing cloth.

Ribbons All Around

Take ribbons way beyond gift wrap to create showstopper decorations.

HAVE-A-BALL ORNAMENTS

Trim the tree with little jewel-tone beauties, or add one to the top of a gift as a keepsake. To make a ribbon ornament, wind raw silk ribbon around a 2- or 3-inch diameter plastic foam ball until completely covered. Secure the end with hot glue. Cut pieces of satin, velvet, or grosgrain ribbon long enough to go around the ball—three pieces for a 2-inch ball and two pieces for a 3-inch ball. Wrap ribbons around ball at equal intervals, securing ends with hot glue at bottom. For tassel, cut and stack three 6-inch pieces of ribbon, knot in center, then glue to bottom of ball. For hanger, cut a 7-inch piece of ribbon, tuck under intersection of ribbons at top of ball, and knot ends.

CARD TRICK GREETING CARD

This easy project is fun to do together with the kiddos. Precut the cardstock and let them choose their favorite ribbons. For a 3×5-inch card, cut one 3×5-inch and one 5×6-inch piece of cardstock. Fold larger piece in half to form card; unfold. Using pencil and ruler, make marks the same widths as ribbons in a triangle shape on right half of card. Use a crafts knife to make slits where marked. Thread ribbon through slits and tape on back. Tape the 3×5-inch cardstock inside the card to hide ribbon ends.

SMOOTH-AS-VELVET NAPKIN RINGS

Bring a little formalwear to the holiday table with bow tie napkin rings that dress up your place settings. To make a ring, cut a 3-inch piece of 1½-inch velvet ribbon. Form a loop and hot-glue the ends together. For bow tie, cut 8 inches of ribbon, form loop, flatten, and hot-glue ends together. Cut a 3½-inch piece of ribbon for center of bow tie. Pinch flattened loop loosely in the middle, wrap cut ribbon around it, and hot-glue ends together in the back. Hot-glue bow tie to the napkin ring.

CROWNING ACHIEVEMENT TREE TOPPER

Contrasting ribbon colors and textures make this layered creation extra impressive.

WHAT YOU NEED

1½-inch-wide turquoise velvet ribbon
1½-inch-wide teal satin ribbon
1½-inch-wide pink satin ribbon
1½-inch-wide teal raw silk ribbon
Cardstock similar in color to ribbons
Peel-and-stick adhesive strips
½-inch-wide pink twill tape
Ruler
Scissors
Hot-glue gun and glue sticks

WHAT YOU DO

1. For bottom layer, cut seven 12-inch-long pieces of velvet, teal satin, and cardstock cut to the same width as the ribbon.

2. Use adhesive strips to sandwich cardstock between one velvet ribbon and one satin ribbon with right sides of ribbons facing out. Repeat with remaining ribbon pairs.

3. Bend a stiffened ribbon and glue ends. Repeat with remaining pieces.

4. Cut a 5-inch cardstock circle. Arrange and layer loops as shown, gluing together and then to cardstock.

5. For middle layer, repeat Steps 1 through 4 using seven 9-inch strips of pink satin and raw silk, gluing circle to bottom layer instead of cardstock.

6. For center bow, wrap a 24-inch piece of twill tape around hand three times. Fan out loops and glue layers together in center. Repeat to make a second ribbon bundle.

7. Wrap short piece of twill tape around center of a bundle and glue ends. Stack bundles and glue together, then to middle layer.

8. Punch small hole in cardstock circle and thread wire through to hang.

ROSETTE WREATH

An updated palette of green, chartreuse, and gold layers works together in this textural wreath.

WHAT YOU NEED

5 to 6 spools of 1- to 2-inch-wide satin, raw silk, and grosgrain ribbon
Measuring tape
Scissors
Fabric pen
Thread
Sewing needle
Pressing cloth
Iron
Hot-glue gun and glue sticks
18-inch-diameter wire wreath form

WHAT YOU DO

1. Cut twenty to twenty-four 36-inch-long strips of ribbon.

2. Starting ½ inch from one end, measure and mark 1-inch intervals about ⅛ inch from edge of ribbon.

3. Thread needle and knot end, leaving a 2-inch tail.

4. Feed needle up through one marker point and down through next. Repeat along length of ribbon.

5. Pull thread to gather ribbon into accordion shape and knot end. Glue ends of ribbon together. Press and twist with hand to form a rosette.

6. Using a pressing cloth, iron flat.

7. Repeat Steps 2 through 6 with rest of ribbon. Hot-glue rosettes to wreath form.

The Creative Home

Let crafting be the centerpiece of Christmastime celebrations—from the joy in creating things together to taking pride in the grand finale.

WRAP IT UP

Let the whole clan join in the fun of wrapping gifts. For a calming effect, limit gift wraps to just a few colors—then enjoy topping the gifts with a variety of looks. Kids can help tape, wrap, make pom-poms, tie bows, and write out tags.

NATURAL BEAUTY

Dress the focal point of the house in glittering finery. Silver, gold, white, and green trims maintain a uniform look on the Christmas tree while almost all of the ornaments are one of a kind. This style tree is great for kids to help trim because anything goes!

№ 1

№ 2

Christmas
Carols

HEAVENLY SNOWFALL

A flurry of snowflakes creates a beautiful wintry effect. Crafted from easy-to-cut coffee filters, these lovely accents snug easily to the wall with a pea-size ball of poster putty.

SUPER SIMPLE

Let a single word say it all. For the picture backing, wrap foam core with linen and insert it into a frame. Spell out a word in cording, pinning it to the foam core to hold it in place. To add to the rustic look, let the interesting patina of slightly tarnished silver reign.

COUNTDOWN CREATION

Make an advent calendar on a linen-backed tackboard. Print numbers on cardstock and trim into tag shapes. Punch holes at the top and accent with round adhesive protectors. Use crafts leftovers, jewelry, and junk drawer treasures to embellish the tags.

ACTIVITY CENTRAL
Designate a table where all kinds of holiday merrymaking can happen—from crafting to wrapping gifts to writing Christmas cards. A chalkboard, framed with a fun pom-pom garland, lets family members share glad tidings every day of the year.

CHILDLIKE WONDER
Give a kid's room a holiday boost with his or her own tree. Add paper and tinsel garlands, a personalized stocking, and festive bedding to let the magic shine.

GO GREEN
Decorate visually without taking up a lot of space. Use fresh greens abundantly to lend instant seasonal flair. Not only does it look festive but it also fills the air with a wintry woodsy scent.

Out of the Woods

The next time you stroll through an antiques store or thrift shop, keep an eye out for wooden items past their prime. You just might stumble onto treasures to repurpose into ultimate holiday decorations.

GREAT CRATE

Large wood containers in any shape make wonderful resting spots for large pinecones and greenery. Adorn the vessel with festive ribbon and this arrangement is holiday ready.

FALLING FLAKES

To make the tree topper stand out, add a second snowflake on top that is painted a solid color. To add to the playfulness of the tree, arrange snowflake "ornaments" so the plaids are at a variety of angles.

TRELLIS TREE

An inverted wooden trellis makes the perfect tree shape to showcase a collection of painted plaid snowflakes. Paint the front of the trellis light green, allowing some of the wood to show through; let dry. To paint wooden snowflakes plaid, use the same technique as for the sign on page 75. Adhere the snowflakes to the trellis using wood glue.

BLODGETT'S
FANCY FULL CREAM
COLBY
CHEESE
C.E. BLODGETT CHEESE BUTTER & EGG CO.
WIS.

HELPFUL HANGER

Vintage wooden hangers, especially those donning advertising, make interesting holders for quilts, towels, and, in this case, a feed sack in holiday hues. To attach it to the hanger, fold the top over the hanger rod and secure with layered buttons.

CLEVER CONTAINERS

For unexpected gift and display boxes, be on the lookout for wooden ones touting red and green advertising. Coordinate ties and trims with the boxes and they get an instant holiday makeover.

PERFECT PEGS

Stockings can be hung on any wall with this clever hanger assembly that is easy to make. Start with a wooden yardstick. Determine how many pegs you need and mark the yardstick in the center to space them out equally. Drill a hole by each mark. Drill a hole into the flat end of a peg. Paint the pegs red or green as desired. Use screws to attach the pegs to the yardstick. Drill a hole near each end of the yardstick for hanging with nails.

STAND-UP SPOOLS

Surprise Santa with his treats resting on large wood spools. To use them for cookies, place a square of waxed paper underneath. The sturdy stands also work wonders to stagger the heights of bottlebrush trees, candles, and figurines.

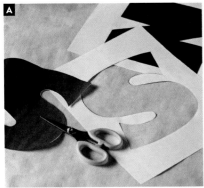

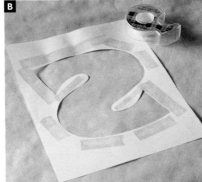

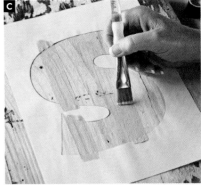

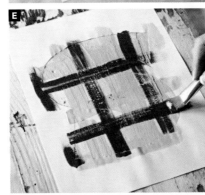

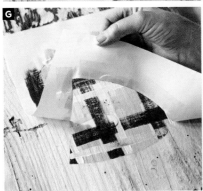

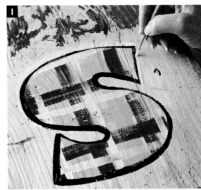

SEASONAL SIGN

The patina of a weather-worn barn board lends the perfect backdrop for a hand-painted sign. Choose a chunky computer font and print out SNOW to fit the size of your board. Cut out the letters, leaving the remainder intact for a stencil as shown in Photo A. Place pieces of two-sided tape around the letter edges as shown in Photo B. Arrange the stencils on the board, leaving room at the top for the rest of the design. Using a wide brush and light green paint, make vertical strokes through each letter stencil as shown on the sample board in Photo C. Add horizontal strokes as shown in Photo D; let dry. Do the same with red paint, placing strokes between the green ones as shown in Photo E. Add white vertical and horizontal strokes using a narrower paintbrush as shown in Photo F; let dry. Remove the stencils as shown in Photo G. Outline each letter with black as shown in Photo H; let dry. Add white highlights to the top and right edges of all letters as shown in Photo I; let dry. Paint "Let" in green at an angle at the top of the sign; let dry. Outline and highlight as for SNOW. Paint "IT" in red; let dry. Outline the letters in black and add white to the center of each letter; let dry. Paint large white snowflake shapes at the top and bottom of the sign.

OPTION (opposite): Use the same technique, on a smaller scale, to embellish a wood crate.

Winter Whites

Decorative items in neutral and fresh shades of white never go out of style, so get crafting with these great ideas in winter white.

PUTTIN' ON THE GLITZ

Love bling? Give a plain wooden tree a bit of glam by adorning it with gold and silver buttons and costume jewelry. To enable the pieces to sit flat, remove any shanks with tin snips. Hot-glue the ornaments to the tree. Use quick-setting gel glue to attach metal leaf beads in gold and silver as shown. Place the tree on a bed of artificial snow under a glass cloche for a magical holiday display.

RING TONES

The holiday wouldn't be complete without a wreath on display, and this two-tone wreath is a cinch to make. Cut approximately two-hundred-eighty 1×16-inch strips of white burlap and tie each one onto a wire wreath form. To finish, wire a complementary neutral-color bow to the top of the fluffy design.

PERFECT POINSETTIAS

Make room for crepe paper poinsettias that will bloom year after year. Trace the pattern on page 154; cut out. Use the pattern to cut bracts and leaves from rolls of ivory and metallic gold crepe paper, tracing so that the paper ridges run through the center of the pattern. For each flower cut two or three small bracts, two or three medium bracts, and five or six large bracts from ivory. In the same manner cut two or three leaves from metallic gold crepe paper.

From florists wire, cut a 5-inch length for each small bract, a 6-inch length for each medium bract, and a 7-inch length for each large bract and each leaf. Run a line of glue along the ridge on the back of a bract and adhere appropriate wire on the glue line, placing the wire end approximately ¼ inch from the bract tip. Repeat for each bract and leaf; let dry.

Gently fold each bract and leaf in half along the wire with wrong sides together. Gently pull on the edges of each piece to create a slightly ruffled effect. Twist bottom edges around wire stems.

Group berry wires together and wrap white florists tape around the wires. Place small and medium bracts around berries, then place large bracts behind; secure with florists tape. Add leaves in the same manner.

SHOW YOUR STRIPES

Transform plain wooden balls into shimmering ornaments for your tree. Paint portions of the balls, masking off desired areas with painters tape, then add glitter to the painted areas. Metallic tape made for fingernail art adds shiny accents to the decorations. Drill a tiny hole at the top and twist in a screw eye to hang with string.

Fun with Felt

Inexpensive and easy to use, felt is a favorite choice for holiday ornaments. Available in endless colors, you can make these darling trims in tones that coordinate with your decor.

PRETTY PARTRIDGES

This Christmas, give your true love this partridge in a Christmas tree. These bird ornaments are built from ivory felt and colorful scraps, and they are a perfect addition to any handmade Christmas ornament collection. Trace the patterns on page 155; cut out. Cut two body shapes and a gusset from ivory felt. Cut plume from red felt. Cut wings and tail from striped felt scarf or sweater. Use needle felt punching tool, following manufacturer's instructions, to needle felt wings into the wide part of the bird body. Use the back side of the punched felt with its smoother finish as the right side. With a ½-inch seam, stitch wrong sides of body and gusset together, easing gusset and body sides together while stitching. Continue around beak, head, and back, and leave an opening for turning. Turn and stuff with polyfill batting then stitch opening closed. Whipstitch tailpiece and plume in place, sew on bead eyes, and add red pearl cotton for hanging.

MINI MITTENS

These sweet petite mittens might not protect your hands, but they will warm your heart with their charming details.

WHAT YOU NEED (For four ornaments)
Freezer paper; pencil; scissors; iron
5×8-inch piece each of crafts felt: mint green, white, red, light blue
Scraps of assorted red-and-white print fabric
White sewing thread
Sewing and embroidery needles
Sixteen ½-inch-diameter buttons: white, red, mint green
Embroidery floss: white, red
Polyester fiberfill
Note: Commercial crafts felt is made of polyester and/or wool. If you use polyester felt, be careful when pressing with a hot iron; the fibers can melt.

WHAT YOU DO
1. Lay freezer paper, shiny side down, over mitten pattern on page 152; trace two mitten shapes for each ornament, leaving ½ inch between tracings. Cut out freezer-paper shapes roughly ¼ inch outside traced lines.
2. Using a hot dry iron, press each freezer-paper shape, shiny side down, onto desired felt color. Lift iron to check that the template is completely (but temporarily) adhered to the fabric. If template is not completely adhered, press again. Let cool. Cut out felt shapes on drawn lines. Carefully peel off freezer paper.
3. Using white sewing thread, sew three buttons to the front of one felt mitten shape as shown in photo.
4. Using two strands of white or red embroidery floss, blanket-stitch two felt mitten shapes together to make a mitten

unit, leaving the cuff end open. To make a blanket stitch, see the diagram on page 157.
5. Stuff the mitten lightly with fiberfill.
6. Cut a 1¼×4¾-inch strip from a red-and-white print fabric scrap. Press under ¼ inch along all edges of the strip. Fold the strip in half crosswise. With the folded strip edge along the thumb side of the mitten unit, sandwich the open mitten cuff edge inside the folded strip; pin. Topstitch the strip a scant ⅛ inch from each edge.
7. Using three strands of white embroidery floss, sew a button to the unfolded end of the fabric strip, stitching through all layers. Knot the floss ends, leaving 2-inch-long tails. Tie the ends of the tails together to form a hanging loop and complete one mitten ornament.

RUSSIAN NESTING DOLL ORNAMENT

Russian nesting dolls, called matryoshkas, come in assorted personalities, but perhaps the most beloved is the motherly peasant figure. This darling little Russian nesting doll ornament makes a great gift, as well as a unique Old World-inspired ornament for your Christmas tree.

WHAT YOU NEED
Water-soluble marking pen
8×9-inch piece of wool or wool-blend felt: turquoise
5×6-inch piece of wool or wool-blend felt: white
Scraps of wool or wool-blend felt: yellow, pink, red, and green
Embroidery hoop and needle
Embroidery floss: black and colors to match felt
Fabric glue
Polyester fiberfill

WHAT YOU DO
1. Trace the pattern on page 155; cut out. Using water-soluble marking pen, trace outlines for two bodies on turquoise felt, one face and one apron on white, one hair shape on yellow, two cheeks on pink, five petals on red, and two leaves on green. Cut out hair, cheeks, petals, and leaves.
2. Embroider the front using two strands of floss for all embroidery. Using marking pen, draw eyes and mouth on face. Backstitch eyes and mouth using black floss. Glue cheeks and hair to face and flower petals and leaves to apron.
3. Referring to the photo, and using split stitches and green floss, outline leaves, make leaf veins, and work two side-by-side rows of split stitches for a stem.
4. Outline just inside cheeks with pink running stitches and just inside flower petals with red running stitches. Add pink French knots between petals for flower center.
5. Cut out face and apron and glue to body front.
6. Referring to photo, outline hair with yellow split stitches and lower portion of face and all around apron with white split stitches. Outline the face and apron again, using turquoise split stitches and placing stitches on turquoise felt.
7. Cut out body front and back.
8. Cut a 10-inch length of turquoise floss and fold it in half to form a hanging loop. Glue ends to wrong side of body back at top of head. Let glue dry. With wrong sides together and using turquoise floss and blanket stitches, sew together body pieces, stuffing shape with fiberfill as you stitch.

SNOW GIFTS

Each of these appliquéd snowmen gets decked out with simple embroidery stitches and colorful felt and fabric embellishments. The snowman patterns are the same; just flip the pattern pieces to make them either right- or left-facing.

WHAT YOU NEED (For four ornaments)

3 2½-inch squares of dark gray felt for backgrounds

3 2½-inch squares of any color felt for backings

9×12-inch piece of white felt for snowmen and candy cane

Scrap of orange felt for noses

Scraps of green felt for hats and wreath

Scrap of light blue felt for ornament

Scrap of print fabric for scarves

Sewing thread: white, green, red, light blue, dark gray

Needles: sewing, embroidery

Water-soluble marking pen

Embroidery floss: black, brown, white, gold, red

3 small red pom-poms

3 6-inch lengths of ribbon for hangers

WHAT YOU DO

1. Trace the patterns on page 156 onto white paper; cut out ⅛ inch outside marked lines. Trace each shape on appropriate felt color or fabric. Cut out shapes on traced lines.

2. Referring to the photo and placement diagram on your pattern, place a snowman on each dark gray felt 2½-inch square; pin. Turn under edges of snowmen ⅛ inch. Using a sewing needle and white sewing thread, hand-appliqué the snowmen to the backgrounds.

3. Position a hat on each snowman's head. Turn under edges ⅛ inch and use white sewing thread to appliqué each hat to head and background. Repeat to appliqué a nose and scarf to each snowman.

4. Using a water-soluble marking pen and referring to the placement diagrams, draw eyes, a mouth, arms, and hands on each ornament. Using two strands of black floss, stitch a French knot for each eye. Use black floss and short running stitches to stitch each mouth. Use three strands of brown floss to backstitch arms and hands (see stitch diagrams on page 157).

5. Position candy cane or wreath above a snowman's raised hand, or position the ornament just below hand. Turn under felt edges ⅛ inch and use matching sewing thread to appliqué edges to background.

6. Use six strands of red floss and straight stitches to form stripes on candy cane.

7. For ornament, use two strands of gold floss to backstitch a stripe at top and bottom of ornament. Use two strands of red floss to make three cross-stitches across center of ornament. Use two strands of black floss to backstitch an ornament hook.

8. Use two strands of gold floss and straight stitches to stitch stripes on wreath. Using one short strand of gold floss, take a small stitch at top of wreath, center stitch on strand, and remove needle. Tie strand in a small bow; trim ends to desired length. If desired, secure center of bow with a small tack stitch.

9. Using red sewing thread, stitch a pom-pom to top of each hat. Use six

strands of white floss to stitch French knots randomly across each background, leaving a ⅛-inch unstitched border around outside edge of background.

10. Pin an embroidered square to a felt backing square. Pin ribbon ends between layers at the top of each ornament. Use dark gray thread to topstitch pieces together, stitching ⅛ inch from each edge.

Glitz in the New Year

Welcome a brand-new year with classy decorations that sparkle as much as the champagne.

TABLE TRIMS

Give each guest a warm fuzzy with a kind saying at his or her place setting. Not having a sit-down style meal? Set the easels randomly on the food or drink table for everyone to enjoy. Paint tiny canvases black; let dry. Use a white marking pen to write the desired message on the canvas, leaving room for decorative ribbon on the left and top. Hot-glue the ribbons in place. Display the mini works of art on easels.

FESTIVE FLUTES

Dollar-store champagne glasses look trés chic with the addition of glittered adhesive initials and fancy gift bags tucked inside. To make the take-home treat bags, cut 12-inch squares of black netting. Place silver-wrapped candy in the center and tie with black cord. Nestle the goodies in the glasses.

EXTRAORDINARY INVITATIONS

Set the tone of your New Year's Eve party with invitations that are as glamorous as the decorations. Use the pattern on page 152 to cut the hat shape from silver print cardstock. Attach the hat to the front of a 4×6-inch card using glue stick. Use hot glue to attach decorative trim to the bottom of the hat. Write "happy new year" on a ½-inch-wide strip of white cardstock; cut to fit hat diagonally. Glue to hat. Cut two 3-inch-square pieces of black netting; accordion fold. Tie the netting in the center with black embroidery floss, leaving long tails. Fluff out the netting and trim edges to be a circle that is approximately 1½ inches in diameter. Hot-glue to tip of hat. Hot-glue a jingle bell in the center. Write the party information on the inside of the card.

RESOLUTION BANNER

Banners liven up living spaces and create a festive environment. For this special occasion, let guests share their New Year's resolutions with fellow partygoers. When guests RSVP, ask them for a resolution or two they wish to share with the group. Write the answers on cardstock triangles and back with silvery paper. Machine-stitch the papers together using ribbon to connect them. The unique banner is sure to inspire as well as to stir up a few giggles.

Lovely Lanterns

NESTLED IN

Here's a great idea for a wreath that hangs on the wall rather than on a door. Place a battery-operated candle in a small lantern with a long handle. Use wire to secure the lantern to the center of a wreath. Top with a flowing ribbon bow and this wreath is ready to shine.

PERSONALLY YOURS

Mini lanterns, available in crafts supply and home decor stores, make extra-special favors. Place a battery-operated votive candle in the lantern, then fill with candy for a sweet take-home gift. Once the candy is gone, the mini light can be hung on the Christmas tree.

QUICK PICK

Holiday picks are inexpensive ready-made accessories for holiday decorating. Choose one that is in scale with the lantern and poke it in, or wire it to, the lantern. Use a battery-operated candle when using picks in lanterns.

JINGLE BELLS ROCK

Nudge an anytime lantern into the holiday season with the addition of glistening jingle bells. Place a candle in the center and gently drop jingle bells around it. For the grand finale, add a ribbon bow with a bell wired to its center.

CENTER OF ATTENTION

Surround a lantern with fresh or artificial greenery for an instant centerpiece. Tuck in wired berries and pinecones to carry out the natural appeal. If needed, wire the pieces together so they remain wreath shaped.

PEPPERMINT STARS
Recipe on page 116

food

Treat holiday guests to a spectacular meal that will truly make the season special. Fabulous roasts, slow-cooker sides, and indulgent sweets create a memorable celebration.

WHITE CHRISTMAS PEPPERMINT LAYER CAKE
Recipe on page 114

A Toast to the Roast

Mouthwatering rubs, glazes, and sauces make these roasts worthy of being the focal point of a holiday table.

HERBED PRIME RIB WITH TWO SAUCES

HERBED PRIME RIB WITH TWO SAUCES

PREP 20 minutes
ROAST 1 hour 45 minutes at 350°F
STAND 15 minutes

WHAT YOU NEED

- 4 tsp. kosher salt
- 1 Tbsp. dry mustard
- 1½ tsp. instant espresso coffee powder
- 1¼ tsp. coarsely ground black pepper
- 1 tsp. granulated garlic or dried minced garlic
- 1 tsp. onion powder
- ½ tsp. dried thyme, crushed
- ½ tsp. dried oregano, crushed
- ½ tsp. ground coriander
- ½ tsp. celery seeds
- 1 Tbsp. olive oil
- 1 4- to 6-lb. beef rib roast
- 1 recipe Merlot Au Jus and/or 1 recipe Horseradish Cream

WHAT YOU DO

1. Preheat oven to 350°F. For dry rub, in a small bowl combine first 10 ingredients (through celery seeds).

2. Rub oil over roast. Sprinkle dry rub over roast; rub in. Using a sharp knife, make six 1×½-inch slits into the fat side of the roast.

3. Place roast, fat side up, in a large roasting pan. Insert an oven-going meat thermometer into center of roast. Roast 1¾ to 2¼ hours or until meat thermometer registers 135°F for medium rare or 2¼ to 2¾ hours or until meat thermometer registers 150°F for medium.

4. Transfer roast to a cutting board. Cover with foil. Let stand 15 minutes before carving. Temperature of the meat after standing should be 145°F for medium rare or 160°F for medium. Slice and serve with Merlot Au Jus and/or Horseradish Cream. Makes 12 servings.

Merlot Au Jus Pour roast drippings into a large glass measuring cup. Skim off fat. Add 1½ cups beef broth, ½ cup Merlot wine, and 2 tsp. Worcestershire sauce. Pour mixture back in pan. Heat and stir until bubbly, scraping up crusty brown bits. If desired, strain jus before serving.

Horseradish Cream In a small bowl stir together one 8-ounce container sour cream, ½ cup mayonnaise, 1 Tbsp. finely chopped green onion, 2 tsp. prepared horseradish, 2 tsp. Dijon-style mustard, 2 tsp. white wine vinegar, and ¼ tsp. kosher salt. Cover and chill until ready to serve.

MUSHROOM-TOMATO-STUFFED PORK LOIN

MUSHROOM-TOMATO-STUFFED PORK LOIN

These spiraled slices of juicy, tender pork are certain to impress your guests.

PREP 40 minutes
ROAST 40 minutes at 350°F
STAND 15 minutes

WHAT YOU NEED

- 1 large portobello mushroom (about 6 oz.) or 2 cups fresh button mushrooms
- 2 tsp. olive oil
- ½ fresh poblano chile, seeded and chopped (about ½ cup)
- ½ cup chopped onion (1 medium)
- 3 cloves garlic, minced
- ¾ cup reduced-sodium chicken broth
- ¼ cup quick-cooking (hominy) grits
- 2 Tbsp. snipped dried tomatoes (not oil-pack)
- 1 1½ to 2-lb. boneless pork loin roast
- ¼ tsp. black pepper

WHAT YOU DO

1. Remove stem from portobello mushroom, if using; if desired, scrape out scales. Chop mushroom. (Or if using button mushrooms, chop mushrooms.) In a large nonstick skillet heat oil over medium heat. Add chopped mushroom, poblano chile, onion, and garlic; cook 5 to 8 minutes or until tender, stirring occasionally. Remove mushroom mixture from skillet; set aside.

2. In the same skillet, bring broth to boiling. Gradually stir in grits; stir in tomatoes. Reduce heat to low. Cook, uncovered, 2 to 3 minutes or until thick, stirring frequently. Remove from heat. Stir in mushroom mixture.

3. Preheat oven to 350°F. Trim fat from roast. Place roast on cutting board with one end toward you. Using a long sharp knife, make a lengthwise cut 1 inch from the left side of the roast, cutting down to about 1 inch from the bottom of the roast. Turn the knife and cut to the right, as if forming the letter L; stop when you get to about 1 inch from the right side of the roast.

4. Open up the roast so it lies nearly flat on the cutting board. Place a large piece of plastic wrap over the roast. Using the flat side of a meat mallet, flatten meat to ¼- to ½-inch thickness. Spread mushroom mixture over meat, leaving a 1-inch border around the edge. Starting from one of the long sides, roll meat around filling. Using 100% cotton kitchen string, tie securely at 1½-inch intervals. Sprinkle meat with black pepper. Place on a rack in a shallow roasting pan.

5. Insert an oven-going meat thermometer into center of meat. Roast, uncovered, 40 to 45 minutes or until thermometer registers 150°F. Cover meat tightly with foil. Let stand 15 minutes before serving. (The temperature of the meat should be 160°F after standing.) Remove string and slice meat to serve. Makes 6 servings.

PORCINI RACK OF LAMB

PORCINI RACK OF LAMB

The earthy taste of the porcini mushrooms complements the natural richness of the lamb.

PREP 30 minutes
ROAST 30 minutes at 425°F, 15 minutes at 475°F
STAND 10 minutes

WHAT YOU NEED
3   large unpeeled shallots
1½ tsp. olive oil
1¼ cups port
2   Tbsp. butter
2   tsp. very thinly sliced garlic
3   Tbsp. all-purpose flour
1   14-oz. can reduced-sodium chicken broth
¼   cup prepared demiglacé
1   tsp. reduced-sodium soy sauce
⅛   tsp. freshly ground black pepper
1   oz. dried porcini mushrooms (1 cup)
1½ tsp. freshly ground black pepper
¾   tsp. salt
3   1- to 1¼-lb. racks of lamb, trimmed

WHAT YOU DO
1. Preheat oven to 425°F. In a small baking dish place shallots; drizzle with oil. Roast, uncovered, 30 minutes or until tender; cool. Peel and cut away root and stem of each shallot.

2. Meanwhile, for port sauce, in a small saucepan bring port to boiling; reduce heat. Simmer, uncovered, 8 to 9 minutes or until reduced to ⅔ cup; remove from pan. In the same saucepan melt 1 Tbsp. of the butter; add garlic and cook 1 minute. Stir in flour; cook and stir 1 minute more or until light golden brown. Gradually whisk in reduced port, the broth, demiglacé, soy sauce, and ⅛ tsp. pepper. Stir shallots into port mixture. Bring to boiling, stirring constantly; reduce heat. Simmer, uncovered, 2 minutes; strain through a fine-mesh sieve. Discard shallots.
3. In a food processor combine dried porcini, 1½ tsp. pepper, and salt. Cover and process to a powder.
4. Arrange oven rack to upper third of oven. Increase oven temperature to 475°F. Sprinkle porcini powder onto all meaty sides of lamb. Arrange lamb on a foil-lined broiler pan, meaty sides up. Roast 15 to 22 minutes or until a thermometer inserted in center of lamb registers 135°F.
5. Transfer lamb to a cutting board. Cover loosely with foil; let stand for 10 minutes. (The temperature of the meat will rise 10°F upon standing.) Meanwhile, in a small saucepan heat port sauce over medium heat until hot. Cut up remaining 1 Tbsp. butter; whisk into hot sauce. To carve racks, cut slices between rib bones. Serve with port sauce. Makes 8 servings.

HOLIDAY HAM

A glossy glazed ham is simple to do and is always a hit. Pick from three glazes—Apricot-Mustard, Pomegranate BBQ, or classic Cranberry-Orange.

PREP 15 minutes at 325°F
BAKE 1 hour 35 minutes

WHAT YOU NEED
1   6- to 8-lb. cooked ham, rump half
1   recipe Apricot-Mustard Glaze, Pomegranate BBQ Glaze, or Cranberry-Orange Glaze

WHAT YOU DO
1. Preheat oven to 325°F. Score ham by making shallow diagonal cuts in a diamond pattern at 1-inch intervals. Place ham on a rack in a shallow roasting pan. Insert an oven-going thermometer into center of ham (thermometer should not touch the bone). Cover with foil.
2. Bake 1¼ hours. Uncover; bake 20 to 60 minutes more or until thermometer registers 140°F. Meanwhile, prepare desired glaze. Brush ham with some of the glaze during the last 20 minutes of baking. Serve with remaining glaze. Makes 20 servings.

Apricot-Mustard Glaze In a small bowl stir together 1 cup apricot preserves, 1 Tbsp. rice vinegar, 1 Tbsp. Chinese-style hot mustard, and 1 tsp. grated fresh ginger or ½ tsp. ground ginger

Pomegranate BBQ Glaze In a medium saucepan cook ½ cup finely chopped onion (1 medium) and 2 cloves garlic, minced, in 1 Tbsp. hot olive oil over medium heat 2 minutes or until onion is tender. Stir in ¾ cup bottled chili sauce, ½ cup pomegranate juice, ¼ cup honey, 1 Tbsp. white or regular balsamic vinegar, ½ tsp. dry mustard, and ¼ tsp. ground black pepper. Bring to boiling; reduce heat. Simmer, uncovered, 20 minutes.

Cranberry-Orange Glaze In a small saucepan combine 1 cup cranberry relish or orange-cranberry marmalade, ¼ cup orange juice, and 1 tsp. snipped fresh thyme or sage. Bring to boiling; reduce heat. Simmer, uncovered, 5 to 10 minutes or until mixture is thickened to a glazing consistency.

HOLIDAY HAM

BACON-WRAPPED
TURKEY

BACON-WRAPPED TURKEY

What makes a crisp-skinned roast turkey even better? Bacon, of course.

PREP 40 minutes
ROAST 3 hours at 325°F
STAND 15 minutes

WHAT YOU NEED

- 10 slices applewood-smoked bacon
- 1 medium onion, finely chopped (½ cup)
- 2 Tbsp. finely snipped fresh sage or 2 tsp. dried sage, finely crushed
- 1 12- to 14-lb. fresh or frozen turkey, thawed if frozen
  Kosher salt and ground black pepper
- 2 to 3 sprigs fresh sage
- 1 medium sweet onion, cut in wedges
  Fresh sage leaves

WHAT YOU DO

1. Preheat oven to 325°F. Finely chop 2 slices of the bacon. Stir together bacon, onion, and sage.

2. Remove neck and giblets from turkey; discard. Rinse turkey; pat dry with paper towels. Loosen the skin from the breast meat by sliding your fingers underneath it, being careful not to tear it. Slide your hand as far as you can toward the opposite end of the turkey, separating the skin from the meat. Rub the bacon mixture underneath the skin over the entire breast, working toward the thighs as much as possible.

3. Sprinkle inside of body cavity with kosher salt and pepper. Fill cavity with sage sprigs and sweet onion wedges. Pull neck skin to back and fasten with a small skewer. Tuck drumstick securely to tail, if available. If there is not a band of skin, tie drumsticks securely to the tail using 100% cotton kitchen string. Twist wing tips under back. Place turkey, breast side up, on a rack in a shallow roasting pan. Sprinkle turkey with additional salt and pepper. Weave remaining 8 strips of bacon in a lattice pattern over the breast. Tuck additional sage leaves into the lattice. Insert an oven-going meat thermometer into center of inside thigh muscles. The thermometer should not touch bone. Cover loosely with foil.

4. Roast 2¾ hours. Remove foil. Roast 15 to 45 minutes more or until thermometer reaches 175°F. (The juices should run clear and drumsticks should move easily in their sockets.) Remove from oven.

5. Cover turkey with foil; let stand 15 minutes before carving. Transfer turkey to a cutting board. Remove and discard onion and sage from inside turkey. Carve turkey.

BACON AND ONION GRAVY

WHAT YOU NEED

- 2 cups turkey broth or reduced-sodium chicken broth
  Butter, melted
- 2 slices applewood-smoked bacon, chopped
- ¼ cup chopped onion
- 1 tsp. snipped fresh sage or ¼ tsp. dried sage, crushed
- 2 tsp. cider vinegar
- ¼ cup all-purpose flour
  Salt and freshly ground black pepper

WHAT YOU DO

1. Stir 1 cup broth into pan drippings from roasted turkey in roasting pan, scraping up any browned bits from bottom of pan. Pour drippings into a 2-cup glass measure. Skim and reserve fat from drippings. If necessary add enough melted butter to the reserved fat to make ¼ cup. Add enough broth to the drippings in measuring cup to make 2 cups total liquid.

2. In a large saucepan cook 2 slices bacon over medium heat until crisp-cooked. Use a slotted spoon to remove bacon from saucepan and drain on paper towels. Reserve 1 Tbsp. bacon drippings in saucepan; add ¼ cup chopped onion and 1 tsp. sage to the mixture. Cook and stir 2 minutes or until onion is tender. Carefully add vinegar to skillet and cook until evaporated.

3. Add the ¼ cup fat to the saucepan with the onion mixture. Stir in flour. Cook and stir over medium heat 1 minute. Add drippings mixture all at once to flour mixture in saucepan, stirring until smooth. Cook and stir over medium heat until bubbly. Cook and stir 1 minute more. Stir in crumbled bacon. Season to taste with salt and pepper. Makes 8 servings.

Make-It-Mine Slow-Cooker Sides

Have it your way with these variations on classic holiday side dishes.

Russet potatoes/Milk/White pepper/ Smoked Gouda/Green onion

Red potatoes/Sour cream/ Crushed red pepper/Feta/Kale

Yukon gold potatoes/Milk/ White pepper/Blue cheese/Spinach

Russet potatoes/Sour cream dip/ Black pepper/Carrots/Monterey Jack

Red potatoes/Buttermilk/ Black pepper/White cheddar cheese/ Cauliflower/Bacon

Yukon gold potatoes/buttermilk/ Ancho chile/Mexican blend/ Frozen whole kernel corn

MAKE-IT-MINE SLOW-COOKER MASHED POTATOES

Fortified with vegetables and made rich and creamy with the cheese of your choice, these mashed potatoes go beyond the basics.

PREP 20 minutes
SLOW COOK 6 hours

WHAT YOU NEED

3   lb. Potatoes, peeled (if desired) and cut into 1-inch pieces
1¼ cups reduced-sodium chicken broth or vegetable broth
½   cup Dairy
¼   cup butter
1   tsp. salt
½   tsp. Pepper
1½ cups Cheese (6 oz.)
1½ cups Vegetables
1   cup crumbled, crisp-cooked bacon (optional)

WHAT YOU DO

1. In a 6-quart slow cooker combine potatoes and broth. Cover and cook on low 6 to 8 hours or on high 3 to 4 hours.
2. Add Dairy, butter, salt, and Pepper. Mash until Potatoes are smooth. Stir in Cheese and Vegetables. If desired, top with bacon.

Shredded white cheddar/Cream of chicken soup/French fried onions and mushrooms/Worcestershire/French fried onions

Shredded cheddar/Cream of chicken with herbs soup/Leeks and crisp-cooked prosciutto/Worcestershire/Sliced almonds

Shredded mozzarella/Cream of onion soup/Red pepper and leeks/Thyme/Gardetto's snack mix

Smoked gouda/Cream of mushroom soup/Bacon and green onions/Rosemary/crackers

Torn American/Cream of onion soup/Red pepper and water chestnuts/Dijon mustard/Potato chips

Shredded provolone/Cream of celery soup/Prosciutto and green onion/Worcestershire/Italian seasoned panko

Serve immediately or keep warm, covered, on warm or low up to 2 hours. Makes 10 servings.

Potatoes (choose one): Round, red, russet, Yukon gold

Dairy (choose one): Buttermilk, milk, Ranch salad dressing, sour cream, sour cream dip

Pepper (choose one or more): Black, cayenne (use only ¼ to ½ tsp.), ground chipotle or ancho chile, crushed red, white

Cheese (choose one or more): Shredded cheddar or white cheddar, Mexican or Italian blend, Monterey Jack, or smoked Gouda crumbled feta or blue (use only 3 oz.)

Vegetables (choose one or more): Shredded carrots; small cauliflower florets; or chopped kale (add the last 30 minutes of cooking Potatoes); frozen whole kernel corn, thawed; sliced green onions (use only 1 cup); shredded spinach

MAKE-IT-MINE SLOW-COOKER GREEN BEAN CASSEROLE

Free up your oven—and time—by creating this traditional dish in a slow cooker.

PREP 20 minutes
SLOW COOK 5 hours

WHAT YOU NEED
    Green Beans
1½ cups Cheese (6 oz.)
1   10.75-oz. can condensed Soup
    Stir-Ins
¼   cup milk
1   Tbsp. Seasoning
    Topper

WHAT YOU DO
1. In a 6-quart slow cooker stir together the first six ingredients (through Seasoning).
2. Cover and cook on low 5 to 6 hours or on high 2½ to 3 hours. Sprinkle with Topper before serving. Makes 12 servings.

Green Beans (choose one): 2 lb. fresh green beans, trimmed and cut into 1-inch pieces; two 16-oz. pkg. frozen cut green beans; five 14.5-oz. cans cut green beans, drained

Cheese (choose one): Shredded cheddar or white cheddar, or smoked Gouda or cheddar, torn American, shredded mozzarella; shredded provolone

Soup (choose one): Cream of celery, chicken, chicken and mushroom, chicken with herbs, mushroom, or onion

Stir-Ins (choose one or more): 8 oz. fresh mushrooms cooked in 2 Tbsp. butter until tender; one 8-oz. can sliced water chestnuts, drained; 1 cup roasted red sweet pepper strips, chopped; 1 cup sliced green onions; 1 cup sliced leeks; ½ cup canned French-fried onions; 6 slices crumbled, crisp-cooked bacon; 6 pieces crisp-cooked prosciutto

Seasoning (choose one): Dijon-style or whole grain mustard; snipped fresh rosemary or thyme; Worcestershire sauce

Topper (choose one): One 6-oz. can French-fried onions, 1½ cups coarsely crushed potato chips, 1½ cups coarsely crushed rich round or rectangular crackers, toasted sliced almonds

Yukon gold potatoes/Chicken broth/
Applesauce/Maple syrup/Bourbon/
Bacon

Parsnips/Chicken broth/Half-and-half/
Granulated sugar/Soy sauce/
Sesame stick crackers and green onions

Celeriac/Apple cider/Milk /
Apple butter/Hazelnut liqueur/
Marshmallow creme and toasted hazelnuts

Carrots/Vegetable broth/Milk/
Honey/Harissa/Leeks and toasted
Sesame seeds

Rutabaga/Veggie broth/Heavy cream/
Molasses/No flavoring/
Chopped almonds and dried cranberries

Sweet potato/Veggie broth/
Buttermilk/Brown sugar/Orange zest/
Candied pecans

MAKE-IT-MINE SLOW-COOKER SWEET POTATO CASSEROLE

Customize the flavors of this sweet and easy vegetable dish to suit the tastes of your guests.

PREP 25 minutes
SLOW COOK 8 hours

WHAT YOU NEED

- 2 lb. sweet potatoes, peeled and cut into 1-inch pieces
- 2 lb. Vegetables, peeled and cut into 1-inch pieces
- 2 cups Liquid 1
- ¾ cup Liquid 2
- 2 Tbsp. butter, cut up
- 2 Tbsp. Sweetener
  Flavoring
- ½ tsp. salt
  Topper

WHAT YOU DO

1. In a 6-quart slow cooker combine the first three ingredients (through Liquid 1). Cover and cook on low 8 to 10 hours or on high 4 to 5 hours. Use a slotted spoon to transfer vegetables to a large bowl, reserving cooking liquid.

2. Mash vegetables until smooth, adding as much cooking liquid as needed. Add the next five ingredients (through salt). Mash until light and fluffy. Sprinkle with Topper before serving. Makes 14 servings.

Vegetables (choose one or more): Carrots, celeriac, parsnips, rutabaga, additional sweet potatoes, Yukon gold potatoes

Liquid 1 (choose one): Apple cider, reduced-sodium chicken broth, vegetable broth

Liquid 2 (choose one): Applesauce, buttermilk (we don't recommend pairing with apple cider), half-and-half, heavy cream, milk

Sweetener (choose one): Apple butter, packed brown sugar, granulated sugar, honey, maple syrup, molasses (use only 1 Tbsp.)

Flavoring (choose one): 1 Tbsp. orange, lemon, or lime zest; 1 to 2 Tbsp. bourbon, hazelnut liqueur, soy sauce, or sriracha sauce, ⅓ cup harissa paste

Topper (choose one or more): 1 cup sliced leeks cooked in 2 Tbsp. olive oil over medium-high heat 8 minutes or until frizzled; 1 cup marshmallow creme; ½ cup chopped toasted almonds, hazelnuts, or walnuts; ½ cup crushed sesame stick crackers; ¼ cup chopped pecans mixed with 2 Tbsp. sugar, 1 Tbsp. softened butter, and 2 tsp. all-purpose flour and baked on a foil-lined baking sheet in a 350°F oven 10 to 12 minutes or until golden; 4 slices crumbled, crisp-cooked bacon; 2 Tbsp. toasted sesame seed; ¼ cup sliced green onions; ¼ cup dried cranberries

MAKE-IT-MINE SLOW-COOKER STUFFING

If you think the stuffing is the best part of the Thanksgiving feast, this recipe offers a bounty of options.

PREP 30 minutes
SLOW COOK 3 hours 30 minutes

WHAT YOU NEED

¼ cup butter
3 cups Vegetables
¼ cup snipped fresh Herb or 2 tsp. dried Herb, crushed
¼ tsp. black pepper
12 cups dry Bread cubes*
1 cup cooked Meat (optional)
1 14.5-oz. can (1¾ cups) reduced-sodium chicken broth, chicken stock, 50% less sodium beef broth, or vegetable broth
¼ cup Liquid
1 cup chopped toasted Nuts (optional)

WHAT YOU DO

1. In a large skillet melt butter over medium heat. Add Vegetables; cook 5 minutes or until tender, stirring occasionally. Remove from heat. Stir in Herb and pepper.
2. Line a 6-quart slow cooker with a slow-cooker liner. Place Bread cubes and, if desired, Meat in prepared cooker. Add vegetable mixture. Drizzle with enough broth and Liquid to moisten, tossing lightly.
3. Cover and cook on low 3½ to 4 hours. If desired, gently stir in Nuts. If needed, stir in enough additional warmed broth to reach desired consistency. Makes 10 servings.

Vegetables (choose a combination): Chopped carrots, fennel, or chestnuts; sliced fresh mushrooms or leeks; finely chopped onion or celery

Herb (choose one or more): Basil, Italian parsley, sage, thyme
Bread (choose one): Ciabatta, corn bread, focaccia, Italian, sourdough, whole grain
Meat (choose one): Crumbled bacon, cubed ham, bulk pork sausage, chopped smoked turkey
Liquid (choose one): Apple juice, hard cider, pear nectar, white grape juice, dry white wine, chicken broth
Nuts (choose one): Almonds, hazelnuts, macadamia nuts, pecans, walnuts
* To make dry bread cubes, cut fresh bread into ½-inch cubes (if using corn bread, cut into 1-inch cubes.) Spread bread cubes in two 15×10-inch baking pans and bake in a 300°F oven 10 to 15 minutes or until dry, stirring twice; cool. (Cubes will dry and crisp as they cool.) Or let cubes stand, loosely covered, at room temperature 8 to 12 hours.

Carrot, chestnuts and onion/Basil/ Crusty whole grain bread/Ham/ White grape juice/Macadamia nuts

Carrot, fennel and leeks/Parsley/ Ciabatta/Smoked turkey/Pear nectar

Leeks, celery and chestnuts/Sage/ Italian bread/Bacon/Apple juice/ Hazelnuts

Onion, mushrooms and celery/Sage/ Corn bread/Sausage/Chicken broth/ Almonds

Mushrooms and leeks/Parsley/ Focaccia/No meat/Wine/Walnuts

Onion, celery and fennel/Thyme/ Sourdough bread/Sausage/ Hard cider/Pecans

Classic Holiday Cutouts

You don't have to be an artist to make cookies that are as fun to look at as they are to eat. Our five best cutout recipes plus easy-to-do decorating ideas are all you need to design inspiring Christmas creations.

LIME WREATHS

These citrusy treats are equal parts tasty and attractive.

PREP 45 minutes
BAKE 11 minutes at 350°F per batch

WHAT YOU NEED

1   cup butter, softened
½   cup sugar
2   tsp. finely shredded lime peel
¼   cup lime juice
1   tsp. vanilla
2¼   cups all-purpose flour
¾   cup finely chopped macadamia nuts

WHAT YOU DO

1. Preheat oven to 350°F. In a large bowl beat butter with a mixer on medium to high 30 seconds. Add sugar. Beat until combined, scraping sides of bowl occasionally. Beat in the lime peel, lime juice, and vanilla until combined. Beat in as much of the flour as you can with the mixer. Stir in any remaining flour and the macadamia nuts. Divide dough in half.

2. On a lightly floured surface, roll one portion of dough at a time until ¼ inch thick. Using a 2½- to 3-inch doughnut cutter or other desired-shape cookie cutter, cut out dough. Place cutouts 1 inch apart on an ungreased cookie sheet.

3. Bake 11 to 12 minutes or until edges are lightly browned. Remove; cool on wire racks. Makes 42 servings.

EVERGREEN WREATH

PISTACHIO WREATH

TREE WREATH

Evergreen Wreath: Spread wreath cookies with green-tinted glaze-consistency Royal Icing (page 111) or Powdered Sugar Icing (page 110). Let stand until dry. Add dollops of icing that is thicker consistency and tinted a darker green. Dab your finger in the thicker icing to give it texture. Sprinkle with green colored sugar. If desired, roll out a red gumdrop and use a very small bird-shape cutter to cut out shapes. Attach with icing.

Pistachio Wreath: Spread each wreath cookie with melted chocolate or Powdered Sugar Icing (page 110); press pistachios into chocolate to adhere. If desired, use a small paintbrush to dust pistachios lightly with gold luster dust (available at crafts stores).

Tree Wreath: Knead green food coloring into dough (for the pictured lime color, knead one drop each of green and yellow gel food coloring into dough). Roll out as directed. Using a small tree-shape or triangle-shape cookie cutter, cut out dough. For each wreath, overlap six to seven tree shapes to create a wreath shape. When cool, use a sieve to dust cookies with powdered sugar. Use frosting to attach small red candies to cookies.

Food

ORANGE-CREAM CHEESE SUGAR COOKIE SNOWMEN

Don't let these cookies brown—bake just until the tops are set and don't look wet.

PREP 30 minutes
CHILL 1 hour
BAKE 7 minutes at 350°F per batch

WHAT YOU NEED

- ½ cup sugar
- 2 tsp. finely shredded orange peel or lemon peel
- ⅔ cup butter, softened
- 3 oz. cream cheese, softened
- ½ tsp. baking powder
- ¼ tsp. salt
- 3 Tbsp. milk
- 1 tsp. vanilla
- 2¼ cups all-purpose flour

WHAT YOU DO

1. In a small bowl combine sugar and orange peel. Press the peel into the sugar with the back of a spoon until the sugar is fragrant and begins to turn orange; set aside.

2. In a large bowl beat butter and cream cheese with a mixer on medium to high 30 seconds. Add sugar mixture, baking powder, and salt. Beat until combined, scraping sides of bowl occasionally. Beat in milk and vanilla until combined. Beat in as much of the flour as you can with the mixer. Stir in any remaining flour. Divide dough in half. Cover and chill 1 hour or until dough is easy to handle.

3. Preheat oven to 350°F. On a lightly floured surface, roll one portion of dough at a time until ⅛ inch thick. Using 2½-inch cookie cutters, cut dough into desired shapes. Place cutouts 1 inch apart on an ungreased cookie sheet.

4. Bake 7 to 9 minutes or until tops are set. Remove; cool on wire racks. Makes 36 servings.

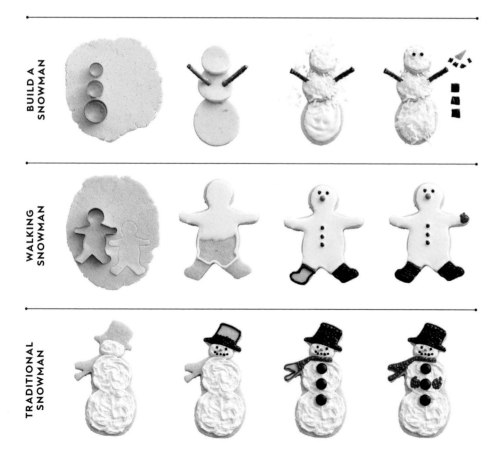

BUILD A SNOWMAN

WALKING SNOWMAN

TRADITIONAL SNOWMAN

Walking Snowman: Prepare and bake dough as directed, using a people-shape cookie cutter to cut out dough. To decorate, spread or pipe glaze-consistency white Royal Icing (page 111) on the body, arms, and head of each cutout. Pipe thicker-consistency black Royal Icing (or use purchased tubes of black frosting) on legs for boots, on middle for buttons, and on head for eyes. If desired, pipe red glaze-consistency Royal Icing on hands for mittens. Add a small orange candy for a nose.

Build A Snowman: Prepare dough as directed using three graduated sizes of round cookie cutters to cut a top, middle, and bottom for each snowman. Slightly overlap the three dough circles on the cookie sheet for each snowman cookie. Bake and cool as directed. Lightly spread white icing or frosting on each cookie; sprinkle with shredded coconut. Use pretzel sticks for arms, licorice pieces for buttons, and assorted candies or colored frosting for eyes, nose, and mouth.

Traditional Snowman: Prepare and bake dough as directed using snowman-shape cookie cutters. Spread face and body of each cookie with Creamy White Frosting (page 111). Pipe black-tinted frosting for hats, eyes, and mouth. Pipe red-tinted frosting for scarf and mittens. Press round black candies into frosting for buttons. If desired, pipe dots of white frosting on buttons.

Round Snowflakes: Prepare dough as directed using a round cookie cutter. Bake and cool as directed. To decorate, pipe or spread glaze-consistency Royal Icing (page 111) onto cookies. Arrange whole almonds, blanched slivered almonds, and pine nuts in desired snowflake designs.

Stacked Snowflakes: Prepare dough as directed using two different sizes of hexagon-shape cookie cutters to cut out equal numbers of shapes. Bake and cool as directed. To decorate, spread or pipe with glaze-consistency Royal Icing (page 111). Let stand until dry. Pipe thicker-consistency Royal Icing in desired snowflake designs on the cookies. Attach a big and small cookie together with icing to create a stack.

Elegant Snowflakes: Prepare dough as directed using a snowflake-shape cookie cutter. Bake and cool as directed. To decorate, spread or pipe with Royal Icing (page 111). Immediately press white chocolate curls into wet icing. Sprinkle with white chocolate shavings and edible pink pearl sprinkles.

ALMOND SUGAR COOKIE SNOWFLAKES

The signature holiday cookie gets all dressed up with almond frosting and delicate decoration.

PREP 1 hour
CHILL 2 hours
BAKE 7 minutes at 350°F per batch

WHAT YOU NEED
1   cup butter, softened
1½   cups granulated sugar
½   tsp. baking powder
½   tsp. salt
2   eggs
¼   cup milk
1   tsp. vanilla
½   tsp. almond extract
½   cup ground blanched almonds
3   cups all-purpose flour
1   recipe Almond Cream Cheese
     Frosting
     Assorted nonpareils and/or colored
     sugars

WHAT YOU DO
1. In a large bowl beat butter with a mixer on medium to high 30 seconds. Add granulated sugar, baking powder, and salt. Beat until combined, scraping sides of bowl occasionally. Beat in eggs, milk, vanilla, and almond extract until combined. Beat in ground almonds. Beat in as much of the flour as you can with the mixer. Stir in any remaining flour. Divide dough in half. Cover and chill 2 hours or until dough is easy to handle.

2. Preheat oven to 350°F. On a lightly floured surface, roll one portion of dough at a time until ⅛ to ¼ inch thick. Using 2½-inch cookie cutters, cut dough into desired shapes. Place cutouts 1 inch apart on an ungreased cookie sheet.

3. Bake 7 to 10 minutes or until edges are very lightly browned. Remove; cool on wire racks. Spread cookies with Almond Cream Cheese Frosting and decorate with nonpareils and/or colored sugars. Makes 48 servings

Almond Cream Cheese Frosting In a medium mixing bowl beat one 8-ounce package softened cream cheese, ½ cup softened butter, and ½ teaspoon almond extract until light and fluffy. Gradually beat in 2 cups powdered sugar until smooth. Gradually beat in 3 to 4 cups additional powdered sugar to make a frosting of spreading consistency.

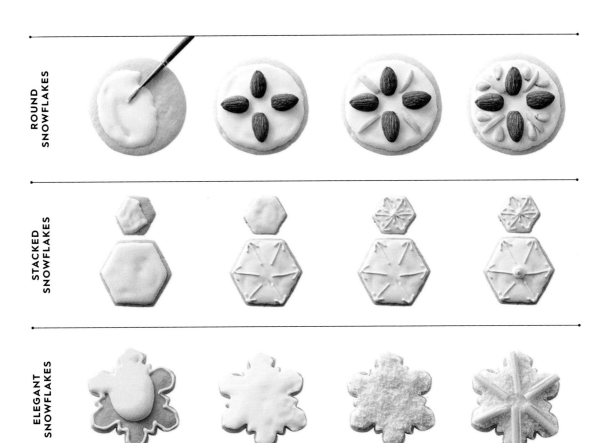

ROUND SNOWFLAKES

STACKED SNOWFLAKES

ELEGANT SNOWFLAKES

GINGERBREAD WOMAN

GINGERBREAD MAN

GINGERBREAD GIRL

Gingerbread Woman: Prepare dough as directed, using woman-shape cookie cutters. Bake and cool as directed. Pipe or spread thick glaze-consistency white Royal Icing (page 111) on cookie for a shirt; attach small red candies for buttons. Pipe green-tinted icing to create suspenders, outline the skirt, and create lines in skirt. Pipe red-tinted icing on head to create hair and in lines between green icing on skirt. If desired, pipe white and green-tinted icing on head to create face.

GINGERBREAD PEOPLE

Keep your gingerbread guys and gals looking dashing with this spirited recipe.

PREP 35 minutes
CHILL 3 hours
BAKE 6 minutes at 375°F per batch

WHAT YOU NEED

½   cup shortening
½   cup granulated sugar
1   tsp. baking powder
1   tsp. ground ginger
½   tsp. baking soda
½   tsp. ground cinnamon
½   tsp. ground cloves
1   egg
½   cup molasses
1   Tbsp. vinegar
2½ cups all-purpose flour

WHAT YOU DO

1. In a large bowl beat shortening with a mixer on medium to high 30 seconds. Add next 6 ingredients (through ground cloves). Beat until combined, scraping sides of bowl occasionally. Beat in egg, molasses, and vinegar until combined. Beat in as much of the flour as you can with the mixer. Stir in any remaining flour. Divide dough in half. Cover and chill 3 hours or until dough is easy to handle.
2. Preheat oven to 375°F. Grease a cookie sheet; set aside. On a lightly floured surface, roll one portion of dough at a time until ¼ inch thick. Using 4½- to 6-inch people-shape cookie cutters, cut dough. Place cutouts 1 inch apart on the prepared cookie sheet.
3. Bake 6 to 8 minutes or until bottoms are lightly browned. Cool on cookie sheet 1 minute. Remove; cool on wire racks. Makes 18 servings.

Gingerbread Man: Prepare dough as directed, using man-shape cookie cutters. Bake and cool as directed. Pipe or spread green-tinted thick glaze consistency Royal Icing (page 111) on cookie to create pants. Pipe thick glaze-consistency red icing on forehead for hair, above pants for a belt, and above belt for buttons. Pipe white icing on feet for shoes, on belt for a buckle, and on head for a face. If desired, pipe green icing on whites of the eyes.

Gingerbread Girl: Prepare dough as directed, using girl-shape cookie cutters. Bake and cool as directed. Pipe or spread glaze-consistency red-tinted Royal Icing (page 111) on cookie to create a dress. Let dry slightly. Pipe white icing on head for face, on the dress for neckline and cuffs, and on skirt to create dots. Pipe green-tinted icing on cookie for a belt and, if desired, on whites of the eyes. If desired, roll a red gumdrop until flat; use a sharp knife to cut out a bow shape. Attach to head with frosting.

ROSEMARY TREES

Don't be put off by the notion of a savory herb in a cookie. You'll be pleasantly surprised by the flavor of this goodie.

PREP 1 hour
CHILL 4 hours
BAKE 8 minutes at 350°F per batch

WHAT YOU NEED

1½ cups sugar
¾   cup slivered blanched almonds
3   Tbsp. fresh rosemary leaves
1   cup butter, softened
½   tsp. baking powder
½   tsp. salt
2   eggs
¼   cup milk
2   tsp. vanilla bean paste or vanilla
½   tsp. almond extract
3   cups all-purpose flour

WHAT YOU DO

1. In a food processor or blender combine ½ cup of the sugar, the almonds, and rosemary leaves. Cover and blend until nuts are finely ground (but not oily) and rosemary is pulverized.
2. In a large bowl beat butter with a mixer on medium to high 30 seconds. Add the remaining 1 cup sugar, the baking powder, and salt. Beat until combined, scraping sides of bowl occasionally. Beat in eggs, milk, vanilla bean paste, and almond extract until combined. Beat in ground almond mixture. Beat in as much of the flour as you can with the mixer. Stir in any remaining flour. Divide dough in half. Cover and chill at least 4 hours or until dough is easy to handle (dough will still be slightly soft).
3. Preheat oven to 350°F. On a well-floured surface, roll one portion of dough at a time until ¼ inch thick. Using a 3- to 4-inch tree-shape cookie cutter, cut out dough. Place cutouts 1 inch apart on an ungreased cookie sheet. If desired, press very small rosemary sprigs onto cutouts.
4. Bake 8 to 10 minutes or just until edges are lightly browned. Remove; cool on wire racks. Makes 36 servings.

POWDERED SUGAR ICING

Just one step and you'll have the perfect icing for your holiday treats.

WHAT YOU NEED

1½ cups powdered sugar
¼   tsp. vanilla or almond extract
3   to 4 tsp. milk

WHAT YOU DO

1. In a small bowl stir together powdered sugar, vanilla, and enough milk to make icing desired consistency.* Makes about ½ cup.

***Test Kitchen Tip:** Add milk, 1 teaspoon at a time, until drizzling or piping consistency is reached. If icing gets too thin, stir in powdered sugar, a spoonful at a time, to rethicken.

PRETZEL TREES

TRIANGLE-TRIO TREES

TEARDROP TREES

Pretzel Trees: Prepare dough as directed using an oval-shape cookie cutter. Bake and cool as directed. To decorate, spread glaze-consistency white Royal Icing (below) in the center of each cookie. Press one small pretzel stick into center of icing. Break three pretzel sticks into pieces. Press them into the icing to look like tree branches. Pipe green-tinted icing onto branches for accents. Use a pastry bag and star tip to pipe yellow-tinted icing stars at tops of trees.

Triangle-Trio Trees: Prepare dough as directed using a triangle-shape cookie cutter to cut dough. On the cookie sheet, overlap three triangles to form a tree. Bake and cool as directed. To decorate, melt green candy coating discs according to package directions. Toss frosted cornflakes with melted candy coating. Spread green icing or frosting on trees. Press coated cornflakes into icing. Pipe dots of red-tinted icing or frosting as accents.

Teardrop Trees: Prepare dough as directed using a scalloped teardrop-shape cookie cutter to cut shapes. Bake and cool as directed. Place icing or frosting into four different bowls; tint frosting in each bowl a different shade of green. Leave frosting in one bowl white. To decorate, spread swaths of each color on each cookie. Break a milk chocolate candy bar into sections. For the trunk use frosting to attach each cookie to a section of chocolate.

CREAMY WHITE FROSTING

This rich and delicious frosting can be used to decorate cookies that require less precise designs.

WHAT YOU NEED

1	cup shortening
1½	tsp. vanilla*
½	tsp. almond extract
1	1-lb. pkg. powdered sugar (about 4 cups)
3	to 4 Tbsp. milk

WHAT YOU DO

1. In a large mixing bowl beat shortening, vanilla, and almond extract with an electric mixer on medium 30 seconds. Slowly add half of the powdered sugar, beating well. Add 2 tablespoons of the milk. Gradually beat in remaining powdered sugar and enough remaining milk to make frosting spreading consistency. Makes about 3 cups.

*Test Kitchen Tip: For a bright white frosting, use clear vanilla.

ROYAL ICING

This icing dries to a hard, glossy finish—perfect for tinting and decorating cookies of all kinds.

WHAT YOU NEED

1	1-lb. pkg. powdered sugar (about 4 cups)
3	Tbsp. meringue powder*
½	tsp. cream of tartar
½	cup warm water
1	tsp. vanilla

WHAT YOU DO

1. In a large bowl stir together powdered sugar, meringue powder, and cream of tartar. Add the water and vanilla. Beat with an electric mixer on low until combined. Beat on high 7 minutes or until stiff. Cover bowl with damp paper towels and plastic wrap while using. Chill remaining frosting up to 48 hours. Makes 5 cups.

Royal Icing Consistency: Royal Icing starts out thick, perfect for piping outlines and accents. To thin the icing for filling in large areas, stir in additional warm water, about ½ teaspoon at a time, until icing is the consistency of a thick, spoonable glaze.

*Test Kitchen Tip: Look for meringue powder in the cake decorating aisle of hobby and crafts stores.

Peppermint Dreams

Fill your dessert plates and platters with pies, cakes, cream puffs, and cookies flavored by this cool, minty, and pretty-in-pink seasonal staple.

PEPPERMINT-FUDGE PIE

PEPPERMINT-FUDGE PIE

This ice cream pie will cut much more easily if you use a sharp knife thats been run under hot water and dried before cutting each slice.

PREP 50 minutes
FREEZE 2 hours
BAKE 10 minutes at 375°F / 475°F

WHAT YOU NEED
Chocolate Crumb Crust
- 1 cup sugar
- 1 5-oz. can (⅔ cup) evaporated milk
- 2 Tbsp. butter
- 2 oz. unsweetened chocolate, cut up
- 1 tsp. vanilla
- 2 pints (4 cups) peppermint ice cream
- ¾ cup sugar
- ½ cup boiling water
- ¼ cup meringue powder*
- 10 striped round peppermint candies, crushed (¼ cup)

WHAT YOU DO
1. Prepare Chocolate Crumb Crust. For fudge sauce: In a small saucepan combine the 1 cup sugar, evaporated milk, butter, and chocolate. Cook and stir over medium heat until bubbly; reduce heat. Boil gently 4 to 5 minutes or until mixture is thickened and reduced to 1½ cups, stirring occasionally. Remove from heat; stir in vanilla. If necessary, beat until smooth with wire whisk or rotary beater. Set aside to cool completely.

2. In a chilled bowl stir 1 pint of the peppermint ice cream until softened. Spread over cooled Chocolate Crumb Crust. Place the cooled fudge sauce in a pastry bag fitted with a round tip about ¼ inch in diameter.** Pipe half of the cooled fudge sauce over ice cream. Freeze 2 hours or until nearly firm. Repeat with the remaining peppermint ice cream and the remaining fudge sauce. Return to freezer while preparing meringue.

3. In a medium bowl dissolve the ¾ cup sugar in the boiling water. Cool to room temperature. Add the meringue powder. Beat with a mixer on low until combined;

beat on high until stiff peaks form (tips stand straight). Fold 3 Tbsp. of the crushed candy into the meringue. Spread meringue over pie, sealing to edge. Freeze 6 hours or until firm.

4. Preheat oven to 475°F. Bake 3 to 4 minutes or just until meringue is light brown. Cover loosely with foil. Freeze 6 to 24 hours before serving. Sprinkle with the remaining crushed candy before serving. Makes 12 servings.

Chocolate Crumb Crust Preheat oven to 375°F. Lightly coat an 8-inch springform pan with nonstick cooking spray; set aside. In a medium bowl combine 1 cup finely crushed vanilla wafers (about 30 cookies), ⅓ cup powdered sugar, and 3 Tbsp. unsweetened cocoa powder. Stir in 3 Tbsp. melted butter. Press crumb mixture firmly into the bottom of the prepared pan. Bake 7 to 8 minutes or until crust is firm. Cool in pan on a wire rack.

*Test Kitchen Tip: Meringue powder is a mixture of pasteurized dried egg whites, sugar, and edible gums. Look for it in the baking aisle of your supermarket or at a specialty food store.

**Test Kitchen Tip: If you do not have a pastry bag, dollop small spoonfuls of the fudge sauce over the ice cream layer.

CHOCOLATE
PEPPERMINT
CREAM PUFFS

CHOCOLATE PEPPERMINT CREAM PUFFS

These dainty treats are an ideal ending to your holiday feast.

PREP 30 minutes
COOL 10 minutes
BAKE 25 minutes at 400°F
FREEZE 15 minutes

WHAT YOU NEED
1	cup water
½	cup butter
¼	tsp. salt
1	cup all-purpose flour
4	eggs
1	tsp. peppermint extract or flavoring
3	cups peppermint stick ice cream
2	oz. bittersweet chocolate, chopped
1	tsp. shortening
2	oz. white chocolate, chopped

WHAT YOU DO
1. Preheat oven to 400°F. Grease a baking sheet. In a medium saucepan combine the water, butter, and salt. Bring to boiling. Add flour all at once, stirring vigorously. Cook and stir until mixture forms a ball. Remove from heat. Cool 10 minutes. Add eggs, one at a time, beating well after each addition. Beat in peppermint extract.

2. Drop dough by rounded teaspoons 2 inches apart onto prepared baking sheets. Bake one sheet at a time 25 minutes (keep remaining dough covered while the first batch bakes). Cool.

3. Cut tops from puffs; remove soft dough from inside. Fill each with ice cream. Replace tops. Place in the freezer to firm, 15 minutes.

4. In a small heavy saucepan, melt bittersweet chocolate and ½ tsp. of the shortening over low heat. Cool slightly. Place melted chocolate in a small resealable plastic bag. Snip off a tiny corner. Drizzle chocolate over puffs. Return puffs to freezer and freeze 5 minutes or until chocolate sets. In another small saucepan melt white chocolate and remaining shortening over low heat; cool slightly. Place in a small resealable plastic bag. Snip off a tiny corner. Drizzle over the puffs. Return puffs to freezer and freeze until serving time. Makes 48 servings.

RED VELVET WHOOPIE PIES WITH PEPPERMINT FILLING

cake layers from pans. Peel off waxed paper; discard. Invert cake layers and cool thoroughly on racks.

5. Meanwhile, prepare the frosting. In an extra-large bowl beat ¾ cup softened butter with a mixer on medium until smooth. Gradually add 2 cups powdered sugar, about ½ cup at a time, beating well. Slowly beat in ⅓ cup milk and the peppermint extract. Gradually beat in remaining powdered sugar. Beat in additional milk to reach spreading consistency. Transfer 2 cups of the frosting to a medium bowl. Add food coloring to make a delicate shade of pink; stir to thoroughly combine.

6. With a long, sharp serrated knife, split each cake horizontally to make a total of four layers. Place one cake layer, cut side up, on a serving plate. Spread top of cake with ⅔ cup of the pink frosting. Repeat with two more cake layers and pink frosting. Top with the last cake layer cut side down. Spread white frosting over top and sides of cake. Decorate as desired with crushed or whole peppermint candies. Makes 12 servings.

RED VELVET WHOOPIE PIES WITH PEPPERMINT FILLING

Steal the show at your next cookie swap with these fluffy treats.

PREP 40 minutes
BAKE 7 minutes at 375°F per batch

WHAT YOU NEED
½ cup butter, softened
1 cup packed brown sugar
2 Tbsp. unsweetened cocoa powder
½ tsp. baking soda
¼ tsp. salt
1 egg
1 tsp. vanilla
2 cups all-purpose flour
½ cup buttermilk
1 1-oz. bottle (2 Tbsp.) red food coloring
1 recipe Peppermint and Cream Cheese Filling
Striped round peppermint candies, finely chopped (optional)

WHAT YOU DO
1. Preheat oven to 375°F. Line a cookie sheet with parchment paper. In a large bowl beat butter with a mixer on medium to high 30 seconds. Add brown sugar, cocoa powder, baking soda, and salt.

WHITE CHRISTMAS PEPPERMINT LAYER CAKE

Frosted with peppermint buttercream and garnished with peppermint candies, this four-layer cake tastes just like Christmas. (Photo on page 91.)

PREP 30 minutes
BAKE 30 minutes at 350°F
COOL 10 minutes

WHAT YOU NEED
2¼ cups cake flour
1 Tbsp. baking powder
1¼ cups whole milk
4 egg whites
1 tsp. vanilla
½ cup butter, softened (1 stick)
1½ cups granulated sugar
¾ cup butter, softened (1½ sticks)
8 cups powdered sugar
⅓ cup milk
2 tsp. peppermint extract
Red or pink food coloring

Peppermint sticks, candy canes, or peppermint candies

WHAT YOU DO
1. For cake: Grease two 8×2-inch round cake pans. Line bottoms with waxed paper; grease paper; lightly dust pans with flour.
2. In a medium bowl stir together flour and baking powder; set aside. In another medium bowl whisk together milk, egg whites, and vanilla; set aside.
3. In a large bowl, beat ½ cup butter with a mixer on low to medium 30 seconds. Add granulated sugar; beat 3 minutes on medium. Alternately add flour and milk mixtures to butter mixture, beating on low after each addition just until combined. Beat 2 minutes on medium. Divide the batter between the prepared pans.
4. Bake in a 350°F oven 30 to 35 minutes or until a wooden toothpick inserted near centers comes out clean. Cool cake layers in pans on wire racks 10 minutes. Run a knife around the sides of the cakes; remove

Beat until combined, scraping sides of bowl occasionally. Beat in egg and vanilla until combined. Alternately add flour and buttermilk, beating on low after each addition just until combined. Stir in food coloring.

2. Drop dough by rounded teaspoons 2 inches apart onto prepared cookie sheet. Bake 7 to 9 minutes or until edges are set. Cool on cookie sheet 2 minutes. Remove; cool on wire racks.

3. Spread Peppermint and Cream Cheese Filling onto bottoms of half of the cookies. Top with remaining cookies, bottom sides down. If desired, sprinkle with peppermint candies before serving. Makes 40 servings.

Peppermint and Cream Cheese Filling In a large bowl combine two 3-oz. pkg. cream cheese, softened; 3 Tbsp. butter, softened; and ½ tsp. peppermint extract. Beat with a mixer on medium until light and fluffy. Gradually beat in 3 cups powdered sugar. If necessary, add milk (1 tsp. at a time) to make a filling of spreading consistency.

DOUBLE-CHOCOLATE PEPPERMINT BISCOTTI

These crunchy cookies have a crunchy peppermint topping.

PREP 45 minutes
CHILL 30 minutes
COOL 1 hour
BAKE 14 minutes at 375°F per batch, 10 minutes at 325°F per batch

WHAT YOU NEED

- ½ cup butter, softened
- ⅔ cup sugar
- ¼ cup unsweetened cocoa powder
- 2 tsp. baking powder
- ½ tsp. salt
- 2 eggs
- 1 tsp. peppermint extract
- 1¾ cups all-purpose flour
- 4 oz. bittersweet chocolate, chopped
- 8 oz. vanilla-flavor candy coating, melted
- ¼ cup crushed peppermint candies

WHAT YOU DO

1. Lightly grease two cookie sheets. In a large bowl beat butter with a mixer on medium to high 30 seconds. Add sugar, cocoa powder, baking powder, and salt. Beat until combined, scraping bowl occasionally. Beat in eggs and peppermint extract until combined. Beat in as much of the flour as you can with the mixer. Stir in any remaining flour and the bittersweet chocolate.

2. Divide dough into four portions. Wrap each portion in plastic wrap or waxed paper. Chill 30 to 60 minutes or until dough is easy to handle.

3. Preheat oven to 375°F. Unwrap each dough portion and shape into a 7-inch loaf. Place loaves 4 inches apart on the prepared cookie sheets; flatten each loaf slightly until about 2 inches wide.

4. Bake, one sheet at a time, 14 to 16 minutes or until a toothpick inserted near centers comes out clean. Cool on cookie sheets on wire racks 1 hour.

5. Preheat oven to 325°F. Using a serrated knife, cut loaves diagonally into ½-inch slices. Place slices cut sides down on cookie sheets. Bake 5 minutes. Turn slices over; bake 5 to 7 minutes more or until crisp and dry. Remove; cool on wire racks.

6. Dip one long side of each cookie into melted candy coating. Place cookies on waxed paper. Sprinkle with crushed candies while coating is still wet. Let stand until coating is set. Makes 42 servings.

SWIRLED PEPPERMINT THUMBPRINTS

The classic thumbprint cookie swaps jam filling for a peppermint swirl.

PREP 30 minutes
CHILL 1 hour
BAKE 10 minutes at 350°F per batch

WHAT YOU NEED

- 2 16- to 16.5-oz. pkg. refrigerated sugar cookie dough
- 1 cup all-purpose flour
- 10 oz. white baking chocolate with cocoa butter, chopped
- ½ cup whipping cream
- ¼ tsp. peppermint extract
  Red food coloring
  White Chocolate Drizzle (optional)

WHAT YOU DO

1. Preheat oven to 350°F. In a large bowl combine cookie dough and flour; knead until smooth. Shape dough into 1½-inch balls. Place balls 2 inches apart on an ungreased cookie sheet. Using your thumb, make an indentation in the center of each ball.

2. Bake in the preheated oven 10 to 12 minutes or until edges are very lightly

DOUBLE-CHOCOLATE PEPPERMINT BISCOTTI

SWIRLED PEPPERMINT THUMBPRINTS

browned. Cool on cookie sheet 1 minute. Remove; cool on wire racks.

3. In a medium bowl combine white chocolate and cream. Microwave, uncovered, on high 1 to 2 minutes or until white chocolate is melted, stirring twice. Stir in peppermint extract. Divide mixture in half. Tint one portion with food coloring. Cover and chill both portions 1 to 2 hours or until mixtures are of spreading consistency.

4. Spoon 1 tsp. of the white chocolate mixture and 1 tsp. of the pink chocolate mixture into the center of each cookie. Gently swirl a knife through mixtures to marble. Let stand until set. If desired, drizzle cookies with White Chocolate Drizzle. Makes 34 servings.

PEPPERMINT PALMIERS

This classic French cookie takes its name from its shape—like palm leaves.

PREP 45 minutes
CHILL 5 hours
FREEZE 4 hours
BAKE 10 minutes at 350°F per batch

WHAT YOU NEED

½ cup butter, softened
½ cup granulated sugar
½ cup packed brown sugar
½ tsp. baking powder
¼ tsp. salt
1 egg
2 Tbsp. white crème de menthe
1 Tbsp. milk
½ tsp. vanilla
2¾ cups all-purpose flour
1 8-oz. pkg. cream cheese, softened
½ cup powdered sugar
¼ cup all-purpose flour
1 Tbsp. white crème de menthe
    Few drops red food coloring
½ cup finely crushed peppermint
    candies

WHAT YOU DO

1. In a large bowl beat butter with a mixer on medium to high 30 seconds. Add granulated sugar, brown sugar, baking powder, and salt. Beat until combined, scraping sides of bowl occasionally. Beat in egg, the 2 Tbsp. crème de menthe, milk, and vanilla. Beat in as much of the 2¾ cups flour as you can with the mixer. Stir in any of the remaining 2¾ cups flour. Divide dough in half. Cover and chill 3 hours or until dough is easy to handle.
2. Meanwhile, for filling, in a medium bowl beat cream cheese, powdered sugar, the ¼ cup flour, and the 1 Tbsp. crème de menthe on low to medium until smooth. Stir in enough red food coloring to tint filling pale pink. Gently fold in crushed candies. Cover and chill up to 2 hours. (Be sure not to chill longer than 2 hours or the candies will bleed into the filling and the filling will become too soft and sticky.)
3. On a lightly floured surface, roll half of the dough into a 12×8-inch rectangle. Spread half of the filling over rolled dough rectangle to within ½ inch of each long edge. Roll up both long edges, scroll fashion, to meet in the center. Brush seam where dough spirals meet with water; lightly press together. Repeat with the

PEPPERMINT PALMIERS

remaining dough and filling. Wrap each roll in plastic wrap; place on a tray or cookie sheet. Freeze 4 to 24 hours or until firm.
4. Preheat oven to 350°F. Line a cookie sheet with parchment paper. Using a serrated knife, cut rolls into ¼-inch slices. Place slices 2 inches apart on the prepared cookie sheet. Bake 10 minutes or until edges are firm and bottoms are light brown. Remove; cool on wire racks. Makes 80 servings.

PEPPERMINT STARS

These melt-in-your-mouth meringues are a relatively healthy cookie choice, given the bounty of sweet treats available this time of year. (Photo on page 90.)

PREP 30 minutes
STAND 1 hour
BAKE 15 minutes at 300°F per batch

WHAT YOU NEED

2 egg whites
½ tsp. vanilla
¼ tsp. cream of tartar
½ cup sugar
¼ tsp. peppermint extract
    Red food coloring (optional)

WHAT YOU DO

1. Place egg whites in a medium bowl; let stand at room temperature 30 minutes.
2. Line two large cookie sheets with parchment paper or foil.
3. Add vanilla and cream of tartar to egg whites. Beat with a mixer on medium to high until soft peaks form (tips curl). Gradually add sugar, 2 Tbsp. at a time, beating until stiff, glossy peaks form (tips stand straight) and sugar dissolves. Quickly beat in peppermint extract. Tint pink with several drops of red food coloring, if desired.
4. Using a pastry tube with a large star decorating tip, pipe cookies onto prepared cookie sheets (form cookies about 1½ inches in diameter). Bake in a 300°F oven 15 minutes. Turn off oven and let cookies dry in oven with door closed 30 minutes. Remove from cookie sheets. Cover and store in a dry place. Makes 45 cookies.

Candy Shop: Quick Chocolate Bark

After melting and spreading the chocolate, it's just top, top, and away!

QUICK CHOCOLATE BARK

Really delicious bark depends on good chocolate, so spring for the best you can afford.

WHAT YOU NEED

1 pound of dark, milk, or white chocolate (avoid chips, which have additives), finely chopped

WHAT YOU DO

1. Place chocolate in a 4-cup glass measuring cup or 1½-quart glass mixing bowl. Pour very warm tap water (100°F to 110°F) into a large glass casserole to a depth of 1 inch. Set the cup or bowl of chocolate into the water, being careful not to splash any water inside. Water should reach halfway up the cup. Every few minutes, gently stir chocolate with a rubber spatula. Change the water as necessary to keep it between 100°F and 110°F. After 15 or 20 minutes it will be melted and ready for making bark.

2. Spread chocolate on parchment paper or waxed paper and top as desired. Let bark set up in a cool room (or, in a pinch, in the fridge). Break or chop into bite-size pieces (or cut into big rectangles with a large knife). (If the bark sets up in the fridge, let it sit 10 minutes at room temp before cutting.)

THE BERRY PATCH
Freeze-dried raspberries + Toasted sliced almonds

THE CAMPFIRE
Smoked almonds + Crushed dried ancho pepper

THE FRUITCAKE
Walnuts + Mixed dried fruit (apricots, cherries, raisins, etc.)

THE TURTLE
Caramel nibs + Toasted pecans

THE SNACK AISLE
Pretzel twists + Ridged potato chips + Peanuts

THE MACAROON
Toasted shredded coconut + Toasted slivered almonds + Sea salt

THE CHRISTMAS TREE
Dried orange-flavor cranberries + Pistachios

THE GINGERBREAD HOUSE
Gingersnap cookies + Crystallized ginger

gifts

MAKE SOMEONE SMILE
Family and friends will never forget gifts
you took the time to make with love.

Clever Kitchen Accents

Table toppers, hot pads, and towels, all decked in festive fabrics, add joy to any kitchen.

HEAT HANDLERS

Hot pads are not only a cooking necessity, but when created with holiday fabrics, they also add a touch of festivity to the kitchen as well. To make one, cut two 9-inch squares of fabric and a 9-inch square of batting. Place fabric squares right sides together and lay the batting square on top. Line up the squares and pin together. Sew a ⅜-inch seam all the way around the square, leaving an opening about 4 inches wide for turning right side out. After sewing, clip off the corners without cutting the stitching. Turn fabrics right sides out with batting in the center. Tuck open ends inside and pin. Press the fabrics to make sure that everything lies flat and then top stitch around the outside edge. If desired, stitch a grid pattern on the hot pad.

HOLIDAY-KISSED TOWELS

In minutes you can transform an ordinary kitchen towel into one that's holiday ready. Cut a 4-inch-wide strip of holiday fabric that is 2 inches longer than the towel is wide. Fold under ¼ inch on each long edge and press. Sew the fabric strip to the towel, ½ inch from the end and folding the excess to the back. Cut a contrasting strip of fabric the same length and 1½ inches wide. Turn under ¼ inch on each long edge and press. Center the fabric strip on top of the first strip and stitch in place.

PIECED TABLE TOPPER

Choose fabrics that coordinate with the gift recipient's decor and this reversible table topper will be a seasonal favorite.

WHAT YOU NEED

Two contrasting holiday fabrics
Cotton batting
6 yards 2½-inch-wide bias strip*
Pins or sewing clips
Coordinating thread
Basting spray or pins
Walking foot recommended

*You can make your own continuous bias strip for binding or purchase it (½ yard of fabric should yield at least 6 yards of 2½-inch-wide bias strip). Once finished, press the bias strip in half lengthwise (wrong sides together) to prep the binding.

WHAT YOU DO

1. Use the pattern on page 156 to cut out 10 wedge shapes from each of the two fabrics. Cut out a center 5-inch diameter circle and a 22-inch diameter backing piece of fabric.

2. With right sides facing and using ¼-inch seams, sew each of the wedge shapes together to create a circle. Iron the seams open. Sew the center circle atop the pieced circle using a zigzag stitch.

3. Spray a small amount of adhesive on the backing fabric, smoothing the batting on top in sections, and then spraying the batting and repeating with the patchwork top. Or, use basting pins to secure the patchwork top, batting, and backing. Baste pieces together.
Note: Use a walking foot for the remainder of the steps.

4. Machine-quilt the table topper as desired.

5. To attach the binding to the top of the quilted place mat, pin the binding along the top edge of the place mat, aligning raw edges. Place a few pins for the first 6 to 7 inches (do not sew here).

6. Begin sewing the binding to the place mat (leaving the 6- to 7-inch tail at the beginning) with a scant ¼-inch seam allowance; backstitch. Go slowly and be careful not to pull or stretch the binding; gently ease the binding along the curve. You should notice some slack on the opposite edge of the binding as you sew. Stop approximately 6 to 7 inches before you reach the opposite end, backstitch and remove the place mat from machine.

7. Pin the remainder of the binding to the edge of the place mat. Trim so there is approximately 1 inch overlapping. Press both ends where they meet in opposite directions. Unpin and place the binding ends right sides together. Stitch along the pressed line to connect the binding. Trim the seam allowance to ¼ inch and press open.

8. Finish attaching the binding to the place mat top by pinning and sewing with a scant ¼-inch seam allowance. Press the binding away from the top of the place mat and make sure that the place mat lays flat and the binding looks smooth.

9. Wrap the binding to the back of the place mat and clip or pin in place. Try to evenly align the binding edge so that it is just past the visible seam (that you just stitched) on the back of the place mat. (NOTE: Sewing clips work wonderfully here, because they hold the binding firmly in place as it is sewn from the top.)

10. Stitch in the ditch or stitch adjacent to the binding edge on the top, making sure that you catch the edge of the binding on the back. Work slowly and stop frequently to check the back. Remove clips as you go. Stitch all the way around the top of each place mat. If you have any areas where the binding is not secured on the back, you can go over them again or stitch the areas by hand.

Make & Take Breads

Whether sweet or savory, homemade bread is always a welcome gift at the holidays. This collection of yeast and quick breads offers something for everyone. Fun, fresh wrapping ideas make them festive and giftable.

GINGERBREAD
LOAVES
Recipe on page 130

FRIENDLY WRAP

A chain of gingerbread folks gives hint to the delight that awaits. To make the band, trace the pattern on page 153 and cut out the shape. Cut a strip of brown kraft paper approximately 3×14 inches. Accordion-fold the paper every 2 inches. Trace around the pattern and cut out through all layers, being careful to leave the hands and feet connected. Unfold the paper and press flat using an iron and pressing cloth. Use paint pens in white and red to detail shapes using the photo as a guide. Wrap bread in cellophane and set into a decorative cardboard bread pan. Wrap the gingerbread band around the bread and tape the ends together underneath.

NATURALLY PRETTY TOPPER

Dress up a wrapped loaf of bread with layered ribbons and cinnamon sticks tied to the top. For a naturally delightful bonus, tuck in a few sprigs of fresh greenery.

**APPLE CINNAMON
BREAD**
Recipe on page 130

CHOCOLATE-ALMOND CROISSANTS

Turn a package of refrigerated crescent rolls into a bakery-worthy treat with almond paste and dark chocolate.

PREP 20 minutes
BAKE 15 minutes at 350°F

WHAT YOU NEED

½   8-oz. can almond paste
¼   cup whipping cream
4   oz. special dark chocolate, chopped
1   8-oz. pkg. (8) refrigerated crescent rolls
1   egg, lightly beaten
1   Tbsp. water
¼   cup sliced almonds
1   Tbsp. powdered sugar

WHAT YOU DO

1. Preheat oven to 350°F. Lightly grease a baking sheet. In a medium bowl cut almond paste into pieces. Add whipping cream to almond paste; beat with a mixer on medium until smooth. Stir in chocolate.
2. Separate dough into eight triangles. Spoon almond paste mixture onto the shortest side of each dough triangle; spread slightly. Starting at the shortest side of each triangle and rolling to the opposite point, roll up dough around filling of each. Curve into crescent shapes and place, pointed sides down, on prepared baking sheet.
3. In a small bowl combine egg and the water. Brush crescents lightly with egg mixture. Sprinkle with almonds.
4. Bake 15 to 17 minutes or until puffed and golden brown. Transfer croissants to a wire rack; cool slightly. Using a sifter or fine-mesh sieve, sift powdered sugar lightly over croissants. Serve warm. Makes 8 croissants.
To Bake Ahead: Prepare and bake as directed; cool completely. Place croissants in a single layer in an airtight container. Cover; seal. Store at room temperature up to 3 days. If desired, reheat before serving. To reheat, preheat oven to 350°F. Arrange croissants on an ungreased baking sheet. Bake 5 to 6 minutes or until warm.

APRICOT, PECAN, AND WHITE CHOCOLATE BREAD

The delicate flavor of this bread is just right for enjoying with a cup of freshly brewed tea.

PREP 25 minutes
COOL 10 minutes
BAKE 1 hour at 350°F

WHAT YOU NEED

½   cup snipped dried apricots
2   cups all-purpose flour
1   cup sugar
1   Tbsp. baking powder
½   tsp. salt
1   egg, lightly beaten
1   cup milk
¼   cup cooking oil
½   cup chopped toasted pecans
½   cup white baking pieces

WHAT YOU DO

1. In a small bowl combine dried apricots and enough boiling water to cover. Let stand 15 minutes; drain.
2. Meanwhile, preheat oven to 350°F. Line a 9×5×3-inch loaf pan with foil, extending foil over edges of pan. Grease foil. In a large bowl stir together flour, sugar, baking powder, and salt. Make a well in center of flour mixture; set aside.
3. In a medium bowl combine egg, milk, and oil. Add egg mixture all at once to flour mixture. Stir just until moistened (batter should be lumpy). Fold in pecans, baking pieces, and drained apricots. Spoon batter into the prepared pan.
4. Bake 60 to 65 minutes or until a toothpick inserted near the center comes out clean. Cool in pan on a wire rack 10 minutes.
5. Use the foil to lift bread out of pan; remove foil. Cool bread completely on wire rack. Wrap and store overnight before slicing. Makes 16 servings.

CHOCOLATE-ALMOND CROISSANTS

APRICOT, PECAN, AND
WHITE CHOCOLATE
BREAD

WREATH ARRANGEMENT

A round green tray sets the stage for this festive presentation.
Line the tray with white parchment paper cut out with pinking
shears. Arrange the croissants spoke style and top with a large
ribbon bow hot-glued to the top of the tray.

BURLAP BEAUTY

Gift recipients will love a plate charger lined with a clear
glass plate to serve their bread in style. Coat a plastic plate
charger with decoupage medium and layer with natural
burlap; flatten with fingers to remove any creases or bubbles.
Let the decoupage medium dry; trim away excess fabric.
Hot-glue trim around the edge and add a bow to one side.
Arrange bread on a glass plate and set onto the charger.
Cover the bread plate with plastic wrap.

HEAVENLY CINNAMON ROLLS
Recipe on page 129

BUTTONED AND BANDED

Trim a baked pan of rolls with banding that makes the gift extra special. Cut a piece of burlap strapping long enough to wrap around pan and overlap 4 inches. On one end, fray 1 inch. Use the pulled-away threads to sew on two large red buttons to the frayed end. Wrap the band around the pan of rolls. Press a piece of adhesive hook-and-loop tape under the buttons and to the strapping below to secure it around the pan. Tie a gift tag to one of the buttons.

BEAUTIFUL BASKET

Line a basket with a lovely cloth napkin and this gift is ready for delivery. To edge the napkin, use simple stitches and embroidery floss to tack on ribbon and rickrack. If rolls will not be used immediately, drop the entire basket of rolls into a cellophane gift bag and tie with a ribbon bow.

HOLIDAY HOUSE BAGS

Transform lunch bags into gift bags. Use a ruler and marking pen to draw windows, a door, a roof, and a wreath on one side of bag. Use red, green, and white paint to add details; let dry. Hot-glue a bow onto the wreath. Place the rolls in a plastic food bag and secure with a wire tie. Set the rolls in the bag. Refold along roofline and tape the flaps to the back.

MULTIGRAIN ROLLS
Recipe on page 129

PEPPERED BACON, GREEN ONION, AND BUTTERMILK SCONES
Recipe on page 130

HEAVENLY CINNAMON ROLLS

The mashed potato in these rolls is the key to their light, fluffy texture.

PREP 55 minutes
RISE 1 hour 15 minutes
BAKE 25 minutes at 375°F
STAND 10 minutes

WHAT YOU NEED
4¼ to 4¾ cups all-purpose flour
1 pkg. active dry yeast
1 cup milk
1 cup mashed, cooked potato
⅓ cup butter
⅓ cup granulated sugar
1 tsp. salt
2 eggs
½ cup packed brown sugar
1 Tbsp. ground cinnamon
¼ cup butter, softened
  Cream Cheese Icing

WHAT YOU DO
1. In a bowl combine 1½ cups of the flour and the yeast; set aside. In a medium saucepan, heat and stir milk, mashed potato, the ⅓ cup butter, the granulated sugar, and salt just until warm (120°F to 130°F) and butter almost melts; add to flour mixture along with the eggs. Beat with a mixer on low to medium 30 seconds, scraping bowl constantly. Beat on high 3 minutes. Stir in as much of the remaining flour as you can.
2. Turn dough out onto a lightly floured surface. Knead in enough of the remaining flour to make a moderately soft dough that is smooth and elastic (3 to 5 minutes total). Shape dough into a ball. Place in a lightly greased bowl; turn once to grease surface of dough. Cover; let rise in a warm place until double in size (45 to 60 minutes).
3. Punch dough down. Turn dough out onto a lightly floured surface. Cover and let rest 10 minutes. Meanwhile, lightly grease a foil roasting pan. For filling, in a bowl stir together brown sugar and cinnamon.
4. Roll dough into an 18×12-inch rectangle. Spread the ¼ cup butter over dough and sprinkle with filling, leaving 1 inch unfilled along one of the long sides. Roll up rectangle, starting from the filled long side. Pinch dough to seal seams. Slice rolled rectangle into 12 equal pieces. Arrange in prepared pan. Cover and let rise in a warm place until nearly double in size (30 minutes).
5. Preheat oven to 375°F. Bake 25 to 30 minutes or until golden. Cool in pan on a wire rack 10 minutes; drizzle with Cream Cheese Icing; cool completely. Makes 12 servings.

Cream Cheese Icing In a mixing bowl, beat 3 oz. of cream cheese; 2 tablespoons butter, softened; and 1 teaspoon vanilla with an electric mixer on medium speed until combined. Gradually beat in 2½ cups powdered sugar until smooth. Beat in milk, 1 teaspoon at a time, to reach spreading consistency.

MULTIGRAIN ROLLS

These hearty rolls make a lovely accompaniment to a bowl of soup—or traditional Christmas Eve oyster stew.

PREP 45 minutes
RISE 1 hour 30 minutes
BAKE 12 minutes at 375°F
STAND 10 minutes

WHAT YOU NEED
3¾ to 4¼ cups all-purpose flour
2 pkg. active dry yeast
1½ cups fat-free milk
¼ cup honey
¼ cup butter
2 tsp. salt
2 eggs
⅔ cup whole wheat flour
½ cup rye flour
½ cup quick-cooking rolled oats
⅓ cup toasted wheat germ
1 Tbsp. cornmeal
  Cornmeal or quick-cooking rolled oats
1 egg, lightly beaten
1 Tbsp. water
  Sesame seeds, poppy seeds, toasted wheat germ, quick-cooking rolled oats, cornmeal, crushed red pepper, and/or garlic-herb seasoning blend

WHAT YOU DO
1. In a bowl combine 2 cups of the all-purpose flour and the yeast. In a medium saucepan heat and stir milk, honey, butter, and salt just until warm (120°F to 130°F) and butter almost melts; add to flour mixture along with the 2 eggs. Beat with a mixer on medium 30 seconds, scraping bowl frequently. Beat on high 3 minutes, scraping bowl occasionally. Stir in whole wheat and rye flours, ½ cup oats, ⅓ cup wheat germ, and 1 Tbsp. cornmeal. Stir in as much of the remaining all-purpose flour as possible.
2. Turn dough out onto a lightly floured surface. Knead in enough of the remaining all-purpose flour to make a moderately stiff dough that is smooth and elastic (6 to 8 minutes total). Shape dough into a ball. Place in a lightly greased large bowl; turn once to grease the surface of the dough. Cover and let rise in a warm place until double in size (1 to 1½ hours).
3. Punch dough down. Turn dough out onto a lightly floured surface. Divide dough into six portions. Cover; let rest 10 minutes. Meanwhile, lightly grease two large baking sheets and sprinkle with additional cornmeal or oats.
4. To shape, divide each portion of dough into four equal portions (to make 24 total portions). Shape each portion of dough into a ball by pulling dough and pinching underneath. Flatten and pull each ball to form a 4×1½-inch oval. Place on prepared baking sheets. Using kitchen shears, make three cuts about ¾-inch deep on each oval. Cover and let rise in a warm place until nearly double in size (30 to 45 minutes).
5. Preheat oven to 375°F. In a bowl, combine the beaten egg and water. Brush tops of ovals with the egg mixture. Sprinkle each with sesame seeds. Bake 12 to 14 minutes or until golden. Remove rolls from pans. Cool on wire racks. Makes 24 servings.

PEPPERED BACON, GREEN ONION, AND BUTTERMILK SCONES

Serve these savory scones with an egg dish for breakfast or brunch or with soup, stew, or a hearty roast for dinner. (Photo on page 128.)

PREP 30 minutes
BAKE 15 minutes at 425°F

WHAT YOU NEED

6   slices peppered bacon
½   cup finely chopped green onions (4)
1   cup buttermilk or sour milk
1   egg, lightly beaten
3   cups all-purpose flour
1   Tbsp. baking powder
¼   tsp. garlic powder
¼   tsp. cayenne pepper or crushed red pepper
½   cup butter
1½ cups finely shredded Gruyère cheese (6 oz.)

WHAT YOU DO

1. In an extra-large skillet cook bacon over medium heat until crisp. Remove bacon from skillet and drain on paper towels. Crumble bacon; set aside. Discard all but 2 Tbsp. drippings from skillet. Cook green onions in hot drippings until tender.
2. Preheat oven to 425°F. Line a large baking sheet with parchment paper. In a bowl whisk together buttermilk and egg; set aside.
3. In a bowl combine flour, baking powder, garlic powder, and cayenne pepper. Using a pastry blender, cut in butter until mixture resembles coarse crumbs. Stir in crumbled bacon, green onions, and cheese. Make a well in the center of the flour mixture. Reserve 2 Tbsp. of the buttermilk mixture. Add remaining buttermilk mixture all at once to flour mixture. Using a fork, stir just until mixture is moistened.
4. Turn dough out onto a lightly floured surface. Knead dough by folding and gently pressing it 10 to 12 strokes or just until dough holds together. Roll out dough evenly to ½-inch thickness. Using a 2- to 2½-inch round cutter, cut rounds from the dough. Place rounds, nearly touching, on prepared baking sheet. Brush rounds with reserved 2 Tbsp. buttermilk mixture.
5. Bake 15 minutes or until golden brown. Transfer scones to wire racks; cool completely. Makes 26 servings.

GINGERBREAD LOAVES

However you like your gingerbread—in cake, cookie, or bread form—this warmly spiced loaf will hit the spot. (Photo on page 124.)

PREP 20 minutes
BAKE 25 minutes at 350°F

WHAT YOU NEED

1½ cups all-purpose flour
1   tsp. baking powder
1   tsp. ground cinnamon
½   tsp. ground ginger
¼   tsp. baking soda
¼   tsp. salt
1   beaten egg
⅓   cup mild-flavor molasses
⅓   cup cooking oil
¼   cup packed brown sugar
¼   cup milk
1   recipe Lemon Icing (see recipe below)
    Chopped crystallized ginger (optional)
    Lemon slice twists (optional)

WHAT YOU DO

1. Grease bottoms and halfway up sides of two 5¾×3×2-inch individual loaf pans.
2. In a medium bowl combine first 6 ingredients (through salt). Make a well in center of flour mixture; set aside. In another medium bowl stir together egg, molasses, oil, brown sugar, and milk. Add egg mixture all at once to the flour mixture. Stir just until moistened (batter will be a little lumpy). Spoon batter into the prepared pans, dividing evenly.
3. Bake at 350°F 25 to 30 minutes or until a wooden toothpick inserted near the centers comes out clean. Cool in pans on wire racks 10 minutes. Remove from pans. Cool completely on wire racks. Wrap tightly and store in the refrigerator up to 3 days or in the freezer up to 1 month.
4. To present, drizzle tops of loaves with Lemon Icing. Decorate with crystallized ginger and a lemon slice twist, if desired. Makes 2 loaves.
Lemon Icing In a small mixing bowl stir together 1 cup powdered sugar and 1 teaspoon lemon juice or vanilla. Stir in milk, 1 teaspoon at a time, until icing is of drizzling consistency, about 5 teaspoons.

APPLE CINNAMON BREAD

Granny Smith apples—the tartest of all widely available apples—are a good choice for this bread.

PREP 35 minutes
BAKE 50 minutes at 350°F

WHAT YOU NEED

3   eggs, lightly beaten
½   cup vegetable oil
½   cup applesauce
2   cups sugar
2   large firm, tart apples, peeled, cored, and shredded
2   tsp. vanilla
3   cups all-purpose flour
1   Tbsp. ground cinnamon
1   tsp. salt
1   tsp. baking power
1   tsp. baking soda
1   cup chopped pecans

WHAT YOU DO

1. Preheat oven to 350°F. Grease bottom and ½ inch up sides and lightly flour two 8×4×2-inch foil loaf pans.
2. In a bowl combine eggs, oil, applesauce, and sugar; beat with a whisk or rotary beater. Stir in apples and vanilla. In another bowl combine flour, cinnamon, salt, baking powder, and baking soda; add to apple mixture. Stir to combine. Stir in nuts. Divide batter between the prepared pans.
3. Bake 50 to 60 minutes or until a wooden toothpick inserted near centers comes out clean. Cool in pans on a wire rack 10 minutes. Remove from pans and cool completely. Wash and dry foil pans. Return cooled loaves to pans. Wrap tightly. Makes 32 servings.

FRESH CRANBERRY SCONES

If you like a little orange with your cranberry, try the variation below.

PREP 20 minutes
BAKE 20 minutes at 375°F

WHAT YOU NEED

2¼ cups all-purpose flour
2   Tbsp. granulated sugar
1   Tbsp. baking powder
¼   tsp. salt
1½   cups fresh cranberries, finely chopped*
2   Tbsp. honey
1   cup whipping cream
1   egg, lightly beaten
1   Tbsp. water
     Coarse sugar

WHAT YOU DO

1. Preheat oven to 375°F. In a bowl stir together flour, the 2 Tbsp. granulated sugar, baking powder, and salt. Make a well in the center of the flour mixture; set aside.

2. In another bowl stir together the cranberries and honey; stir in whipping cream. Add cranberry mixture to flour mixture all at once. Using a fork, stir just until moistened.

3. Turn dough out onto a lightly floured surface. Knead dough by folding and gently pressing it 10 to 12 strokes or until dough is nearly smooth. Dough may appear pink. Pat or lightly roll dough into an 8-inch square. Cut into nine squares. Place squares about 1 inch apart on an ungreased baking sheet. In a bowl stir together the egg and the water. Lightly brush wedges with egg mixture and sprinkle with coarse sugar.

4. Bake 20 to 25 minutes or until tops are golden brown. Remove scones from baking sheet; cool completely. Place scones in a tall plastic container. Makes 9 servings.

Fresh Cranberry-Orange Scones: Prepare as above, except stir 1½ tsp. finely shredded orange peel into the cranberry mixture.

FRESH CRANBERRY SCONES

MERRY MUGS

Holiday mugs make the perfect containers for a few servings of scones. Place a food-safe plastic bag into the mug and fill with scones. Use a wire tie to secure the bag closed. Thread narrow ribbon through a medium-size jingle bell and tie around the bag top. Tuck in a sprig of artificial holly and berries to complete the wrap.

A Stitch in the Nick of Time

Crochet your way through the holidays with thoughtful gifts that are a cinch to make.

WISE GUY

Whooooo's ready to get organized while looking stylish? Work up this owl basket in rounds of half double crochet, then crochet each eye piece and sew the pieces to the body. Embroider the beak using yarn and a tapestry needle.

WHAT YOU NEED

Two 5-oz. skeins worsted weight yarn: gray
Size J crochet hook
Blunt-end yarn needle
Gauge:
6 rows and 8 hdc = 3 inches
A glossary of crochet abbreviations is at the end of the instructions.

WHAT YOU DO

Crochet the Basket:
Note: The basket is worked in a spiral, so joining rounds is not necessary. Mark beginning of each round.

Rnd 1: With 2 strands of yarn held together, ch 3 (2 chs counts as hdc), hdc 7 times in beg ch (8 hdc).
Rnd 2: Hdc-inc in each st (16 hdc).
Rnd 3: *Hdc-inc, hdc in next st; rep from * 7 more times (24 hdc).
Rnd 4: *Hdc-inc, hdc in next 2 sts; rep from * 7 more times (32 hdc).
Rnd 5: *Hdc-inc, hdc in next 3 sts; rep from * 7 more times (40 hdc).
Rnd 6: *Hdc-inc, hdc in next 4 sts; rep from * 7 more times (48 hdc).
Rnd 7: *Hdc-inc, hdc in next 5 sts; rep from * 7 more times (56 hdc).
Rnd 8: *Hdc-inc, hdc in next 6 sts; rep from * 7 more times (64 hdc).
Rnds 9-17: Hdc in each st around (64 hdc).
Rnd 18: *Hdc-dec, hdc in next 6 sts; rep from * 7 more times (56 hdc).

Rnd 19: *Hdc-dec, hdc in next 5 sts; rep from * 7 more times (48 hdc).
Rnd 20: *Hdc-inc, hdc in next 5 sts; rep from * 7 more times (56 hdc).
Rnds 21-26: Hdc in each st around (56 hdc). Sc in next st, sl st in next st to finish off. Fasten off, and weave in ends.

Make the Eyes:
Note: Each eye is worked in a spiral, so joining rounds is not necessary. Mark the beginning of each round.

First Eye
Rnd 1: With 2 strands of yarn held together, ch 2 sc 6 times in beg ch (6 sc).
Rnd 2: *Sc 2 times in each st; rep from * 5 more times (12 sc).
Rnd 3: *Dc 2 times in each st; rep from * 11 more times (24 sc).
Rnd 4: *Dc 2 times in next st, dc; rep from * 5 more times, tr, dtr, picot; fasten off.

Second Eye
Rnds 1-3: Rep First Eye instructions.
End 4: Picot, dtr, tr, * dc, dc 2 times in next st; rep from * 5 more times, hdc, sc, sl st to finish off eye; fasten off and weave in ends.

Add Eyes to Basket:
Position the right eye on the basket at the point of the last st. Using two strands of yarn and a tapestry needle, tack down the center of the eye; using the center hole as a guide, bring the needle up through the center and then back down in the first round of stitches. Continue until the center is secure.
Using two strands of yarn and the outside stitches of the eye, tack down the eye securely, leaving the picot stitches unsewn. Weave in all ends. Repeat with left eye.

Add the Beak:
Using two strands of yarn and long straight stitches, embroider a beak between the bottoms of the eyes.

CROCHET ABBREVIATIONS:

beg beginning
ch chain
dc double crochet
dtr double treble
hdc half double crochet
inc increase
lp loop
rep repeat
rnd(s) round(s)
sc single crochet
sl st slip stitch
st(s) stitch(es)
tr treble crochet
yo yarn over
hdc-inc, dc-inc, sc-inc work two of the designated st in one stitch
hdc-dec (Yo, insert hook in next st, yo and draw up a lp) twice, yo and draw through all 5 lps on hook
picot ch 5, sl st in top of first st

FASHION FAVORITE

All your gal friends will love the go-with-everything style of this crossover button scarf. By crocheting with four strands of yarn at once, you quickly give shape to the scarf in just eight rows.

WHAT YOU NEED

Two 5-oz. skeins worsted
    weight yarn: green
Size P crochet hook
Blunt-end yarn needle
Two large buttons
Gauge:
7 sts and 4 rows=4 inches in dc
Finished Size: 7½×35 inches

WHAT YOU DO

Crochet the Scarf:

Note: Use both ends of each skein of yarn to work with four stands throughout the pattern.

Ch 63.

Row 1: Dc in 3rd ch from hook (counts as dc), dc in each ch (60 dc): ch 3, turn.

Row 2: Dc in each dc (60 dc); ch 3, turn.

Rows 3–8: Rep Row 2.
Fasten off and weave in ends. Sew buttons through both layers where desired.

STRESS RELIEVER

Filled with a lavender sachet, this flexible crocheted neck roll is perfect for soothing sore muscles. The exterior is a crocheted rectangle that's stitched together along the sides to form a wrap for holding the sewn sachet. Pop it in the microwave on high for a minute for extra comforting power.

WHAT YOU NEED

Two 4×11½-inch pieces of muslin
Filler, such as dried lavender, flaxseed, or rice
Worsted weight yarn: ivory
Size I crochet hook
Tapestry needle
Two ¾-inch-diameter buttons in ivory
Finished Size: 4½×10½ inches

WHAT YOU DO

Sew the Sachet:

1. With right sides facing, sew the 4×11½-inch pieces of muslin together, leaving one of the short sides open.
2. Fill the sachet with your choice of filler through the opening. Hand-stitch the opening closed.

Crochet the Cover:

Note: Gauge is not critical to the success of the project.

Ch 32.
Row 1: Sc in 2nd ch from hook; *sk next ch, ch 1, sc in next ch; rep from * across; ch 1, turn (16 sc, 15 ch).
Row 2: Sk first st, *sc in ch-1 sp, ch 1, sk next st; rep from * across. End with a sc in turning ch from precious row; ch 1, turn (16 sc, 15 ch). Rep Row 2 until piece measures approximately 10½ inches square. Fasten off and weave in ends.

Assemble the Neck Roll:

1. Fold up the bottom third of the crocheted cover and use a tapestry needle and yarn to sew short side seams on two layers, leaving the top third loose as a pocket flap.
2. Sew two buttons to front of pocket, spacing each approximately 2½ inches from side edges. Insert pillow into pocket and fold the top third of cover down. Fasten buttons in the openings between stitches on the flap.

THERAPEUTIC NECK ROLL FILLERS

Dried Lavender
Known for its pleasing scent, lavender promotes relaxation.

Flaxseed
When microwaved, flaxseed provides prolonged moist, dry heat.

Rice
Use rice as a cheap, yet short-lived, filler for heat or cold.

Put Your Stamp On It

FRAME WORTHY

Postage stamps, especially vintage ones, many times offer a set of related themes. The holiday collection (printed from the Internet) is just right to back with retro style Christmas scrapbook paper. To carry out the look, frame the mini piece of art using an old cardboard photo frame trimmed with ribbon and a button.

FILL 'EM UP

Paper party cups become even more special when touting a scallop-edge postage stamp. Old or new, holiday stamps add interest and really stand out when backed with black paper trimmed close to the scallop.

SO CHARMING

Slipped into a charm frame, postage stamps become showy jewelry. Back the stamp with contrasting paper to define the intricate edge.

MERRY MESSAGES

Don't just save your holiday cards, save their envelopes too! Cut out the upper right corner from the envelope and trim into a tag shape. Glue the shape to holiday paper and trim leaving a border. Punch a hole through the end, and thread with ribbon, and this fun package topper can deliver holiday greetings or state the gift recipient.

SECOND TIME AROUND

Even postmarked postage stamps have a beauty about them. Use a glue stick to attach them to white cardstock and affix to folded scrapbook paper place cards. Add guest's names and these little treasures are ready to dress up the table.

kids

READY FOR FUN

Like the elves in Santa's workshop, kids will be happy all day long making decorations and gifts that deliver holiday joy.

Filter Fun

Coffee filters—inexpensive crafting supplies—become glorious with zaps of color from food dyes and marking pens.

VIBRANT FLAKES

All snowflakes are different and this holds true for these fun-to-make flakes bursting with color.

WHAT YOU NEED
Large paper coffee filters
Iron
Baking pan with lip
Waxed paper
Liquid food coloring in assorted colors
Water in spray bottle
Plastic gloves or tweezers
Scissors
Pressing cloth

WHAT YOU DO

1. On an ironing board, iron coffee filters flat as shown in Photo A. Adults should assist or do this step for young children. Unplug iron.

2. Line a baking pan with waxed paper. Stack up to three flattened filters on the waxed paper. Squeeze drops of food coloring onto the filters as shown in Photo B.

3. Using spray bottle, wet the filters just enough to soak through layers and let the colors bleed into one another as shown in Photo C.

4. Wearing plastic gloves or using tweezers, carefully peel layers apart and place on sheets of clean waxed paper to dry as shown in Photo D. Let the filters dry thoroughly.

5. For each snowflake, fold filter in half as shown in Photo E. Fold in half three more times as shown in Photo F, until a pie shape is achieved.

6. Use scissors to cut out pieces to make a snowflake shape as shown in Photo G. Keep some of the folded areas uncut so the snowflake doesn't fall apart.

7. Carefully unfold the filter as shown in Photo H. Carefully press the snowflake flat, if needed, between layers of waxed paper and pressing cloths to avoid getting color on the cloths.

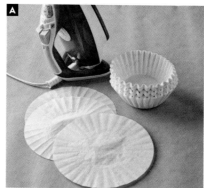
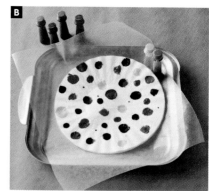
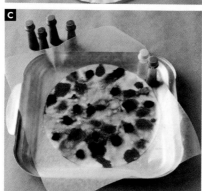
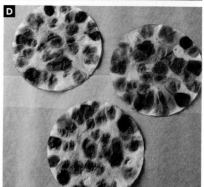
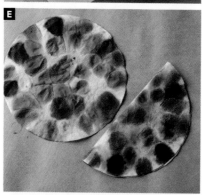
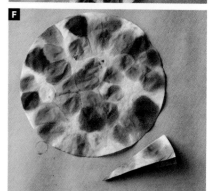
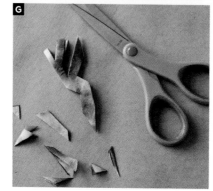

PACKAGE POINSETTIAS

In lieu of bows, let the kids make feathery poinsettias to grace gifts. To make one, iron five large paper coffee filters flat (adults should help young children). Fold each filter into a pie shape, as shown for snowflake on page 140. Holding the point, cut the opposite end into a rounded leaf shape. Vary the length of petals as shown in photo, left. Unfold the shapes and lay them singly on a waxed paper-lined pan with a lip. Put a few drops of food coloring into ¼ cup water; pour into a clean spray bottle; spray shapes until there is color throughout. Let the filters dry and carefully remove from waxed paper. Arrange the layers largest to smallest and staple an X in the center. Put hot glue in the center of the poinsettia and drop 14-inch-diameter wood beads into the glue. (For young children, use white glue.) Fluff out the poinsettia by gently pulling apart the layers. Secure to package using double-sided tape.

QUICK FAVORS

Lightweight yet strong, coffee filters are easy for older kids to stitch into a mini Christmas stocking. To make one, iron two large paper coffee filters flat. Copy the pattern on page 157 and cut out. Use pattern to cut the shape from each filter. Use marking pens to draw zigzags or other designs on the cuff. Thread a sharp embroidery needle with floss; knot one end. Use running stitches to sew the layers together, stitching approximately ¼ inch from the edge.

TINY CHERUBS

Create darling heaven-sent angels. To make a gown, twist the center of a large paper coffee filter as shown in Photo A. Fill a small glass half full with water and add a few drops of food coloring. Holding the filter by the twisted end, dip it in the colored water until the color soaks up to the twist as shown in Photo B. Use two colors if desired, dipping half in one color and the remainder in the second color. Remove the filter from the glass immediately and place on a disposable plate. Use a paintbrush to dab the edge with food coloring to create an ombre look as shown in Photo C. Let the filter dry. Use a marking pen to draw a simple face on a 1-inch wood bead. Shape hair from pipecleaners and glue to bead; let dry. Add a metallic gold pipe cleaner halo. Dip the twisted end of the filter into glue and tuck it into the bead; let dry.

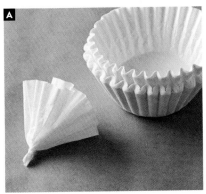

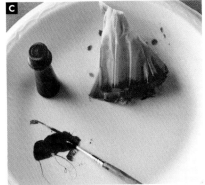

Just for You

Kid-friendly projects, designed for gift giving, come with a lesson in recycling.

CARD COLLECTOR

Once a tissue box, this cheery container keeps Christmas cards organized.

WHAT YOU NEED
Empty facial tissue box
Scissors
Packing tape
Wrapping paper
Wide black ribbon
Strong double-sided tape
Letter stickers
2-inch-square piece of cardboard
White yarn
Darning needle
Red jingle bell
Small paper punch

WHAT TO DO
1. Make cuts in the box top from the center to each corner as shown in Photo A. Cut off any plastic from the top.
2. Use packing tape to secure the flaps to the inside of the box as shown in Photo B.
3. Cut a wrapping paper piece large enough to wrap around box and cover at least half of the inside sides as shown in Photo C.
4. Wrap the box using packing tape to secure as shown in Photo D.
5. Cut a piece of black ribbon to wrap around the entire box. Secure the ends to the box back as shown in Photo E.
6. Use sticker letters to spell out "merry" or another holiday word on the front of ribbon as shown in Photo F. Add dot accents, if desired.
7. Cut ¾-inch V notches on opposite sides of 2-inch-square of cardboard. Wrap 50 times with yarn as shown in Photo G.
8. Cut a 24-inch length of yarn. Double the yarn and tie tightly around yarn at notches as shown in Photo H.
9. Thread a yarn tail through the needle and through the jingle bell. Remove the needle and knot yarn ends to secure jingle bell to center of yarn loops as shown in Photo I.

10. Use scissors to clip yarn loops to make a pom-pom as shown in Photo J. Leave two tails long.
11. Use a paper punch to make two holes about 1 inch apart in the upper left corner of box as shown in Photo K.
12. Thread one yarn tail onto the needle and poke through one hole in box. Do the same with the remaining yarn tail. Knot the yarn ends on the inside of the box to attach the pom-pom as shown in Photo L.

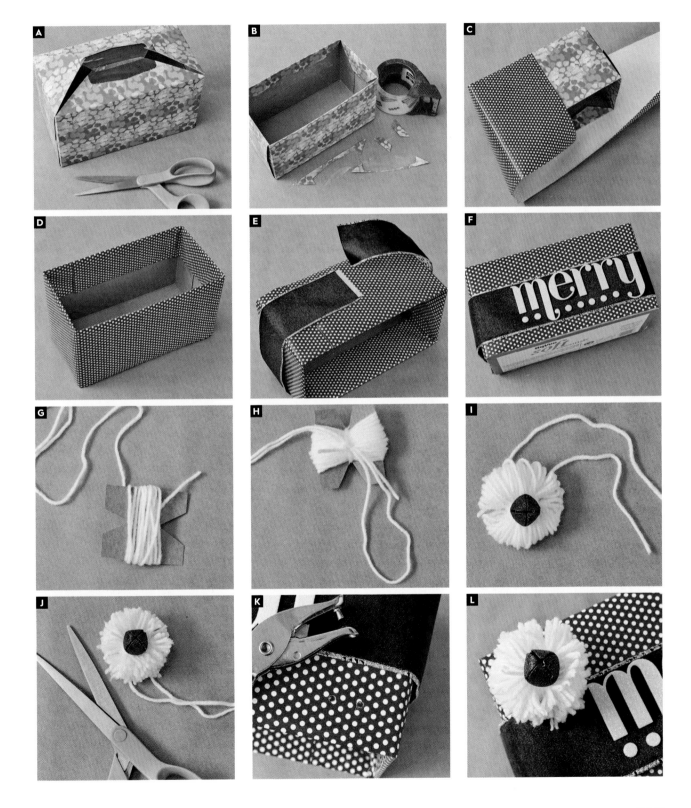

kids

TOOTHPICK CADDIES

Merry snowmen, crafted from pill bottles, make cheery decorations and serve up toothpicks as a bonus.

WHAT YOU NEED

Clean pill bottle

Plastic cap that fits bottle lid (such as from food containers or hair products)

Hot-glue gun and glue sticks

Spray paint: white, black

Scrap of orange felt

Scissors

Toothpick

Acrylic paint: black

Fabric scrap or ribbon

Sprig of artificial greenery

Small jingle bells

WHAT YOU DO

1. Hot-glue the plastic cap, open side up, onto the pill bottle lid as shown in Photo A.

2. In a well-ventilated work area, spray-paint the bottle bottom white and the lid black as shown in Photo B.

3. Cut a tiny triangle nose from orange felt. Glue onto bottle, approximately 1 inch from the top. Dip a toothpick in black paint and dot two eyes and a smile around the nose as shown in Photo C.

4. Cut a strip of fabric or ribbon to fit around lid as shown in Photo D. Hot-glue in place.

5. Glue greenery sprig and jingle bells to the rim as shown in Photo E.

6. Cut a scarf piece from fabric or ribbon, fringing the end. Tie around snowman as shown in Photo F.

ANTARCTICA ORNAMENTS

Before you toss out a liquid hand soap dispenser, you may want to think twice. These penguin pals are a great way to repurpose those shapely plastic bottles.

WHAT YOU NEED

Empty and clean plastic hand soap dispenser
Black spray paint
Acrylic paint: black, white, blue, orange
Paintbrush
Marking pen cap
Pencil eraser
Toothpick
Red felt
Scissors
4-inch piece of wire
Small pom-pom
Metallic silver pipe cleaner
Adhesive gems
Ribbon

WHAT YOU DO

1. Remove the lid from the soap dispenser and pull off the spout. In a well-ventilated work area, spray-paint the bottle black and let dry. Paint a white heart shape for the penguin head as shown in Photo A.
2. Paint the body and a scalloped bottom as shown in Photo B; let dry.
3. Dip the open part of a marking pen cap into black paint. Press onto top of heart shape as shown in Photo C to indicate the outline of the eyes. Let the paint dry.

4. Dip the pencil eraser into blue paint and dot inside eye outlines as shown in Photo D.
5. Paint an orange beak and let dry. Dip the toothpick into white paint and dot eyes and beak as shown in Photo E. Let dry.
6. Twist cap back onto bottle as shown in Photo F. Using the cap height as a gauge, cut a rounded triangular piece from felt to make a hat shape that covers the bottle cap. Twist the ends of the wire together.

7. Hot-glue the felt onto the bottle cap, inserting the wire loop at the top as shown in Photo G.
8. Trim the cap with pom-pom, adhesive gems, and pipe cleaner as shown in Photo H. Glue on a small ribbon bow below the beak.

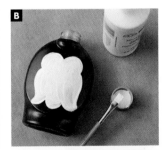

TREAT-FILLED SNOW GLOBES

Clear plastic ornaments rest in dolled-up cardboard ribbon spools to make extra-fun snow globes.

WHAT YOU NEED

Empty cardboard ribbon spool
Acrylic paint: silver, green
Paintbrushes
Large clear plastic ornament with removable hanger
Adhesive gems and snowflakes
Assorted trims, such as ribbon and beaded thread
Hot-glue gun and glue sticks
Scissors
Small white candies
Resealable plastic bag
Small rubber band

WHAT YOU DO

1. For the base, tear off one end of the ribbon spool and sand any rough edges as shown in Photo A.

2. Paint the base silver as shown in Photo B. Let the paint dry.

3. Hanger end down, paint a simple tree shape on the ornament as shown in Photo C; let dry.

4. Press gems onto the tree to resemble ornaments as shown in Photo D.

5. Trim the base as shown in Photo E, using hot glue when needed.

6. Pour candies into the ornament to resemble snow on the ground. Cut a 2-inch-diameter circle from sandwich bag as shown in Photo F. Place the circle over the ornament opening and secure with the rubber band. Set the globe into the base.

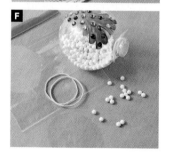

For Santa and Crew

In the season of giving, these crafts offer thanks to the jolly man in red and his guys in green.

TREAT TRAY
A plate charger makes a wonderful tray to serve Santa some cookies and milk. To trim it, hot-glue decorative trim or braid around the rim. Use stickers to add festive details.

SWEETS TO GO
Whether left for Santa's elves or given to friends during the holiday season, these merry bags are sure to be appreciated. Fill decorative paper bags with wrapped candies and fold the bag top over; seal with a dimensional sticker. Tuck in a sprig of artificial holly.

A Pressing Matter

MERRY MESSAGES

This year let the kids make the greeting cards, thank yous, and invitations. Stamped pieces instantly jazz up the front of plain note cards. Add a stamped message and the fun creation is ready to be mailed.

COOL WRAPS

Rubber stamps and ink pads provide hours of fun for kids and make holiday gift wrap extra special. To make paper ribbon, stamp sheets of white cardstock and cut into strips. Tape strips together for larger packages. Use a tag-shape punch to make blank tags. Personalize the tags using letter stamps.

CREATIVE CHAINS

Turn kids loose with white paper and rubber stamps and they'll have a blast making paper chains. After stamping sheets of cardstock, cut them into 1×6-inch strips. Use double-sided tape to secure the ends as the links are connected.

JOLLY BAGS

Transform plain bags into super-cute seasonal sensations. Use a variety of stamps and ink colors, pressing some stamps horizontally and some vertically to fill the paper. Cut out two ovals to make a snowman. Cut a top hat from black paper. Cut a triangular nose and a hat band. Use glue stick to adhere the ovals and nose to black paper; trim a narrow border. Glue the shapes together and to the bag front.

FESTIVE RINGS

No need to spend money on napkin rings when this free version is so much fun. Make use of tubes from wrapping paper, toilet paper, and paper towels. Cut tubes into 1½- to 2-inch-long pieces and use double-sided tape to adhere stamped paper strips.

patterns

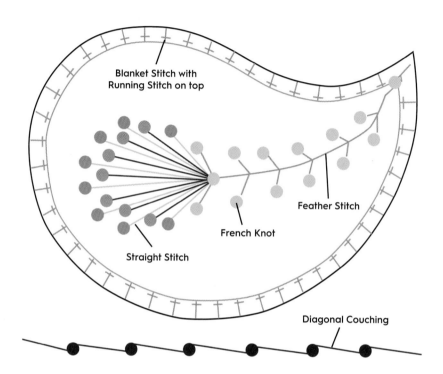

Blanket Stitch with
Running Stitch on top

Feather Stitch

French Knot

Straight Stitch

Diagonal Couching

AUTUMNAL GREETING
PAISLEY
page 8
Full-Size Pattern

MINI MITTENS
page 81
Full-Size Pattern

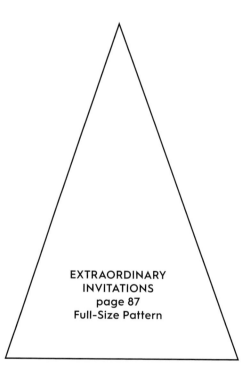

EXTRAORDINARY
INVITATIONS
page 87
Full-Size Pattern

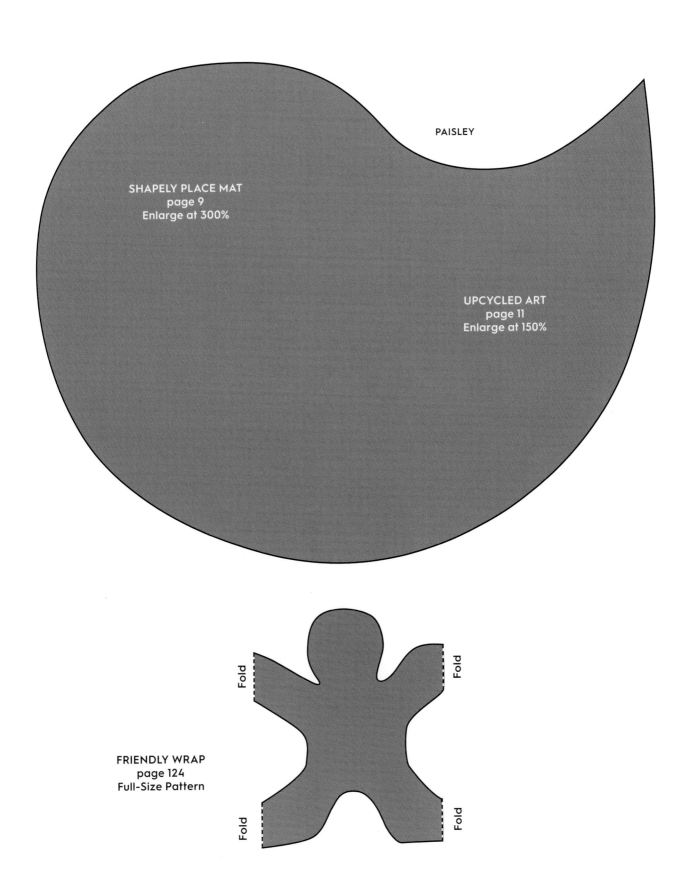

PAISLEY

SHAPELY PLACE MAT
page 9
Enlarge at 300%

UPCYCLED ART
page 11
Enlarge at 150%

Fold

Fold

Fold

Fold

FRIENDLY WRAP
page 124
Full-Size Pattern

Patterns

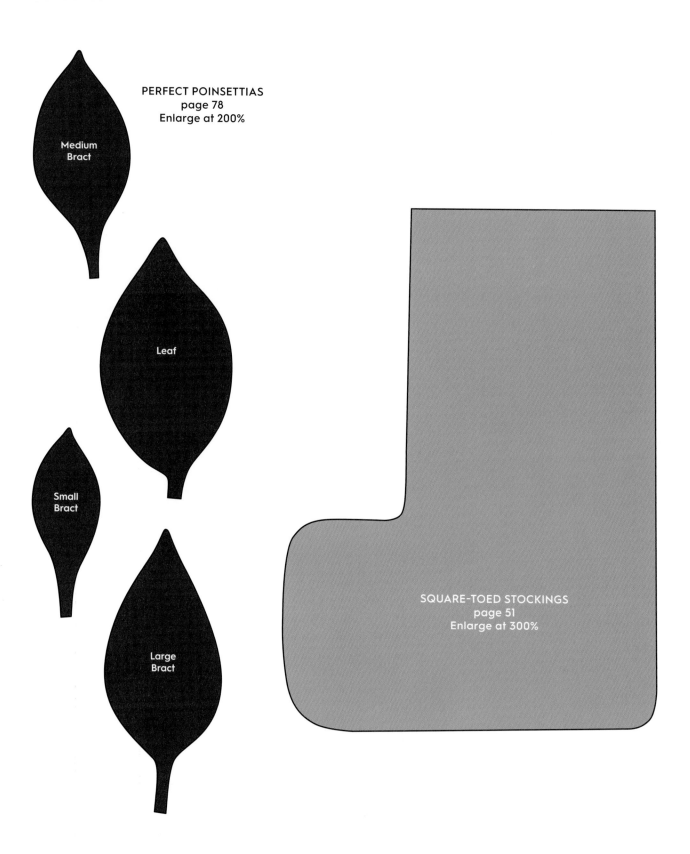

PERFECT POINSETTIAS
page 78
Enlarge at 200%

Medium
Bract

Leaf

Small
Bract

Large
Bract

SQUARE-TOED STOCKINGS
page 51
Enlarge at 300%

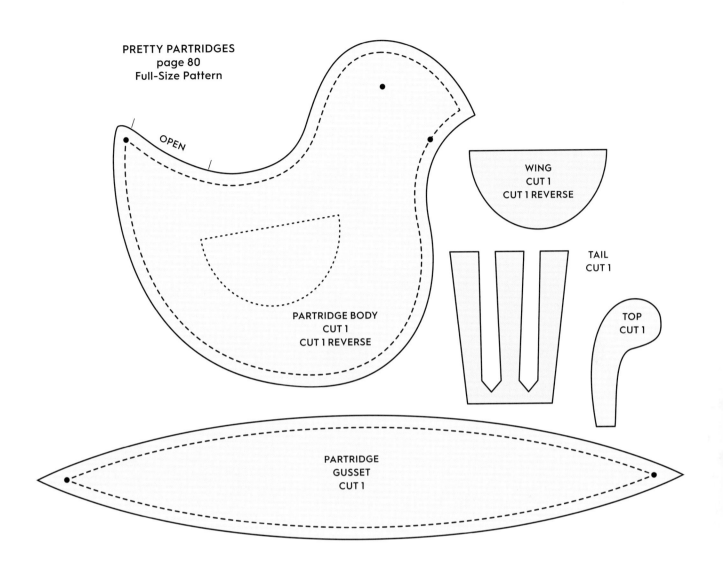

PRETTY PARTRIDGES
page 80
Full-Size Pattern

OPEN

PARTRIDGE BODY
CUT 1
CUT 1 REVERSE

WING
CUT 1
CUT 1 REVERSE

TAIL
CUT 1

TOP
CUT 1

PARTRIDGE
GUSSET
CUT 1

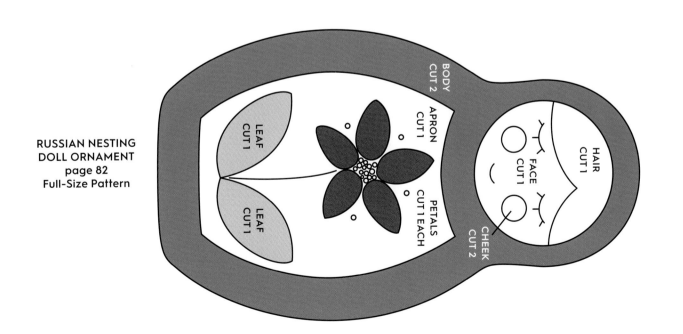

RUSSIAN NESTING
DOLL ORNAMENT
page 82
Full-Size Pattern

BODY
CUT 2

LEAF
CUT 1

LEAF
CUT 1

APRON
CUT 1

PETALS
CUT 1 EACH

FACE
CUT 1

HAIR
CUT 1

CHEEK
CUT 2

Patterns

SNOW GIFTS
page 83
Full-Size Patterns

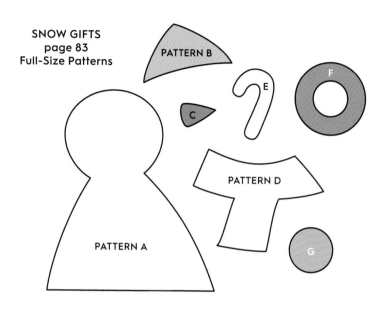

PATTERN B

E

C

F

PATTERN D

PATTERN A

G

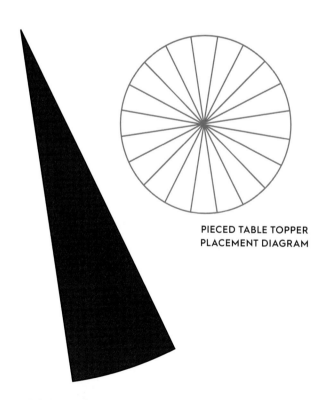

**PIECED TABLE TOPPER
PLACEMENT DIAGRAM**

PIECED TABLE TOPPER
page 122
Enlarge wedge pattern
at 300%

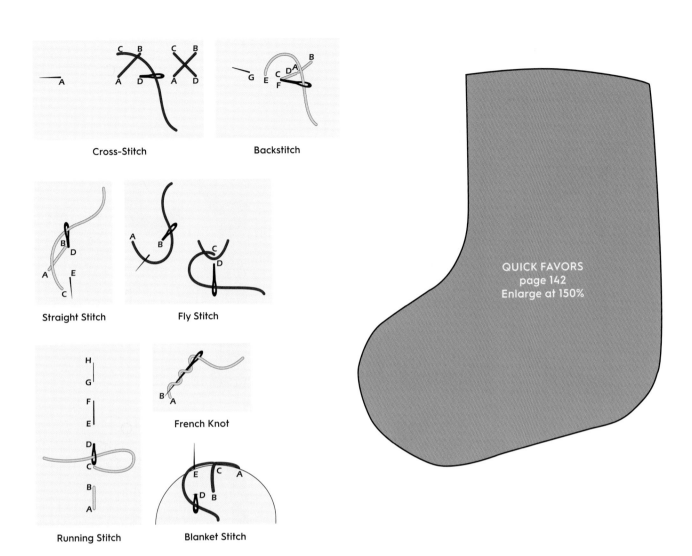

Cross-Stitch

Backstitch

Straight Stitch

Fly Stitch

French Knot

Running Stitch

Blanket Stitch

QUICK FAVORS
page 142
Enlarge at 150%

GOOD TOSS
page 53
Enlarge at 200%

DEaR SaNTa

Patterns

ADORABLE APPLIQUÉ
page 49
Enlarge at 200%

DEAR SANTA

index

Index

CREDITS

Photo Styling
Sue Banker
Doug Samuelson

Photography
Jason Donnelly
Jacob Fox
Marty Baldwin